WRITING PROCESS ACTIVITIES KIT

WRITING PROCESS ACTIVITIES KIT

75 READY–TO–USE LESSONS AND WORKSHEETS FOR GRADES 7–12

Mary Lou Brandvik

THE CENTER FOR APPLIED RESEARCH IN EDUCATION
West Nyack, New York 10995

10   9   8   7

Some material in this book appeared in *The Process of
Writing: A Seminar Approach,* © 1986 by Mary Lou
Brandvik. Used here by permission.

Library of Congress Cataloging-in-Publication Data

Brandvik, Mary Lou.
    Writing process activities kit : 75 ready-to-use lessons and
worksheets for grades 7–12 / Mary Lou Brandvik.
        p.   cm.
    Includes bibliographical references.
    ISBN 0-87628-968-5
    1. English language--Composition and exercises--Study and teaching
(Secondary)   2. Creative writing (Secondary education)   I. Title.
LB1631.B763   1990
808'.042'0712--dc20   90-32268
                                                                        CIP

ISBN   0-87628-968-5

THE CENTER FOR APPLIED
RESEARCH IN EDUCATION
BUSINESS & PROFESSIONAL DIVISION
A division of Simon & Schuster
West Nyack, New York 10995

Printed in the United States of America

To Paul, David, and Ahna, whom I love
more than chocolate, and to my students,
who have written so willingly and powerfully.

About the Author

Mary Lou Brandvik was born in Reeder, North Dakota, and spent her early school years in Hollywood, California, before returning to North Dakota. She graduated *summa cum laude* from Concordia College in Moorhead, Minnesota, with a BA in English and Art. She attended the University of Wisconsin and earned a Master's degree in English Education from the University of Illinois. She has taught in public schools in Illinois and Minnesota as well as at Bemidji State University. She has led in-service workshops in Minnesota and was a participant in the Northern Minnesota Writing Project. Ms. Brandvik chaired the Bemidji Public Schools' Writing Curriculum Committee and was selected "Teacher of the Year" in the Bemidji Public Schools in 1988.

About This Resource

The *Writing Process Activities Kit* places in your hands a complete, sequential program of lessons, worksheets, and reproducible writing samples that you can use to introduce your students to the writing process. It was designed by an experienced English teacher to make the instruction of writing easier for you and the learning of writing easier for your students. It will encourage you to make writing the heart of your English classroom. It will also help you to teach listening and speaking skills and to incorporate minilessons on mechanics and usage as they apply to student writing.

Although the 75 lessons here call for students to write more, they will not increase your paper load, because you will be spending more time earlier guiding and conferring with each student as a piece of writing evolves. In addition, students will themselves learn editing skills and how to respond to one another's work.

Part One of the book introduces the writing process and explains the workshop setting as it may be used in the junior high or high school classroom. It also includes a discussion of prewriting techniques and presents options for responding to and grading student writing. (If you are already familiar with the writing process and ways to apply it in the classroom, you may wish to skip ahead to Part Two.)

Part Two contains detailed unit plans for 75 lessons which may be followed in their entirety or incorporated into other teaching plans. The lessons are accompanied by reproducible sample student writings, checklists, and worksheets.

The type of writing called for in most of the lessons is primarily personal narrative, although a complete poetry unit is also included. The writing experiences offered here serve as an excellent foundation for understanding and practicing the writing process and lead easily to continued writing with an emphasis on fiction, exposition, or research. Appendices at the end contain additional writing suggestions, including possible assignments in literature classes and across the curriculum and ways to utilize computers in your writing workshop.

Students enthusiastically support this approach to writing and, by overcoming their suspicions and fears about writing, make an excellent beginning.

> This class has helped me a lot in learning how to express myself in a completely new way for me. I have never attempted to write before, other than what I had to do or what was assigned. It's fun to write, especially when you get comments on what is both good and what can be changed. I'm not nearly as embarrassed to read my writ-

ings out loud because everyone seems to read theirs without being forced to.

Bill

I feel I can write more openly because of this class. It's taught me not to be afraid to write!

Kris

I never did like writing before this class, but I found out if I write something I want to write about, it is fun.

Lori

About writing, Flannery O'Connor has said, "Anyone who has survived to the age of eighteen has enough material to last them the rest of their lives." The workshop setting and an understanding of the writing process make writing more satisfying and less painful for students and more rewarding and less time consuming for teachers.

The writing workshop is a structure that permits basic instruction and remediation as well as enrichment. It permits individual growth while allowing for group work. It develops confidence in students and acknowledges accomplishment. It becomes magical, and that is what good teaching is all about.

Mary Lou Brandvik

Table of Contents

part one

THE WRITING PROCESS AND THE ELEMENTS OF THE WRITING WORKSHOP

chapter *I*

THE WRITING PROCESS

Writing is one of the most demanding tasks our students face. Recently, however, much has been discovered about how successful writing happens at the school level.[1] Teachers and researchers have come to realize that any writing project can be separated into several steps or phases of work. This approach, known as the *writing process,* makes even the most challenging writing assignment more manageable and satisfying for students and allows us to be effective and successful teachers of writing.

When writing is studied as a process, it has a number of distinct stages. At the simplest level, these include **prewriting, drafting, revising, and presenting** (or publishing).[2]

PREWRITING

Prewriting is the time when a writer plays with ideas and gathers information to prepare for the actual drafting. It may involve reading, talking, or simply thinking about a topic. Sometimes it includes an incubation period when thoughts are allowed to coalesce without conscious attention. In real-life situations it can extend for weeks or even months.

Classroom activities, designed to help students gather as much information as possible to draw on during the drafting stage include

> Drawing
> Observing
> Listening
> Reading
> Note taking
> Discussing

---

[1] Some outstanding sources concerning the writing process and devoted primarily to the elementary student include Donald Graves, *Writing: Teachers and Children at Work* (Portsmouth, NH: Heinemann, 1983), and Lucy Calkins, *The Art of Teaching Writing* (Portsmouth, NH: Heinemann, 1986). A source which focuses on junior high age students is Nancy Atwell's *In the Middle; Writing, Reading, and Learning with Adolescents* (Montclair, NJ: Boynton/Cook, 1987). Tom Romano's *Clearing the Way: Working with Teenage Writers* (Portsmouth, NH: Heinemann, 1987), is useful for teachers working with high school writers.

[2] There is a danger in assuming there is only one process when, in fact, there are many. Writers do not all work alike. However, students need to understand that writing is a several-stage process, and if they try to do all the stages at once, they are unlikely to be successful.

Listing
Brainstorming
Rehearsing
Outlining (rough)
Clustering (mapping or webbing)
Visualizing
Freewriting

In addition, students also may be encouraged to keep journals and use them for recall and topic ideas.

The amount of time spent at this point in writing varies from activity to activity and writer to writer. While it is helpful for students and teachers to distinguish between the stages of the writing process, it is also important to recognize that writing is actually recursive, not linear.[3] Writers may plan, then write, then revise. They may also revise, plan some more, then write again. A student may proceed, for example, to the drafting stage only to discover he or she needs to return to the prewriting stage for more information.

Prewriting is also the point when students begin to clarify the topic, the format, the audience, and the time.

TOPIC- Is the writing topic to be imposed by the teacher, or will students be free to choose their own or at least be allowed to pick from many options? "I can't think of anything to write" is a complaint familiar to all of us, yet good planning on our part can help a student generate so many ideas that he or she will feel a *need* to write.

FORMAT- Is the writing to be a sentence, a paragraph, a theme, a journal entry, a letter, a poem, a research paper? Does the student understand the possibilities and characteristics of each?

AUDIENCE- For whom is the student writing? Will he or she be expected to deliver the writing to its intended audience? Frequently, students write only for teachers. However, a variety of authentic audiences serves as motivation for students to revise and edit, and positive responses from real audiences encourage them to write again.

TIME- How much time will be devoted to this project? Will the student be expected to complete the writing outside class, or will class time be allocated for discussion, for drafting, for revising? Will the student be expected to share a draft with other students? It *is* important to design writing experiences so students have plenty of time to write and revise in class.

---

[3] Janet Emig, *The Web of Meaning* (Montclair, NJ: Boynton/Cook, 1983), p. 140.

Students need guided practice in their writing and in their understanding of the writing process. It is also crucial that students not be allowed to submit early drafts as finished pieces of writing.

DRAFTING

Drafting is the stage when the writer begins recording ideas in rough form. Getting started on paper is often difficult and may produce many false starts and discarded openings. "How should I begin?" is a question familiar to all teachers. We need to remind our students that a first draft is simply a time to gather, explore, and discover ideas and is not expected to be a final, polished writing. No one need be concerned with neatness, editing, or mechanical correctness in the earliest draft.

Sometimes furnishing a student with a first sentence is all that is necessary to get the drafting stage going. The technique of **freewriting** (also called "sprint writing" or "rush writing") is ideal for any writer beginning a first draft. In freewriting students write nonstop, capturing as many ideas as possible. They jot down, words, phrases, or sentences rapidly. Ideas, coming with great speed and momentum often trigger other ideas along the way, and ideas are the goal of the earliest draft.

Your role at this time is to give plenty of guidance and encouragement and to be stingy with criticism. Ideally, you will also write with the students and serve as a role model. Students gain confidence when they realize that all writers make false starts, that the struggle at this point is usually typical of all writing.

REVISING

Revision is an ongoing activity which is part of every stage of the process. Even in prewriting, a writer sorts, chooses, and critiques ideas.

Once a first draft is completed, writers begin to revise ("to see again"). They consider the content and ask themselves if the ideas and purpose are clear to an audience. They become concerned about the *effect* of the writing. Early changes will involve ideas and their sequence; later drafts may be concerned with combining sentences and making paragraph adjustments.

When writers have taken a draft as far as they are able, they need time for others to respond to it. They share the draft with their peers and/or the teacher, listening to their responses and acting on them. As students respond to one another's writing, their editing skills develop enormously.

Later drafts involve polishing the writing to present in final form to a particular audience. Editing for mechanics in the final stage of the writing is approached more willingly by students, because they begin to feel like successful writers. They are proud of their ideas and wish to present them in the best possible way.

Initially, students often believe they are hopeless writers when they can't get their writing perfect immediately. As they work through and understand the writing process, they come to understand that most writers rework and revise extensively.

PRESENTING (OR PUBLISHING)

This is the stage most often omitted from school writing. Frequently, it is only the teacher who reads and grades a student's writing. However, when students are expected to write for and deliver their final drafts to real audiences, they are highly motivated to write again.

Possible audiences for student writers are other students, other teachers, parents, relatives, principals, cooks, custodians, pen pals, authors, politicians, or famous people. Student writing may be presented in school displays or published in school-produced newspapers, anthologies, or homemade booklets. Students may submit writings to literary contests, professional publications, or local newspapers. The presentation of writings as gifts to trusted adults for special occasions is as popular with older students as with younger ones.

A Note on Research

Many researchers and teachers have come to believe that students learn to write best by performing real tasks: stories, poems, letters, notices, or reports for real audiences. They also emphasize that spelling and vocabulary are best learned in context, that sentence building is more productive than either sentence analysis or labeling. They agree that drill on isolated skills may be useful for students when diagnosis shows weaknesses in specific areas (and you'll notice these quickly as you work with individual writers), but it is not a good substitute for whole writing tasks.[4] Whenever possible, minilessons for practice in skill building are included in the following lesson designs.

Another important thread that runs through the studies of the writing process is the recognition that errors are often a natural part of learning, and understanding error is significant in the process approach to the teaching of writing. Thus the revision stage of writing is highly important. By encouraging students to take a constructive role in analyzing and evaluating their own and the writing of their peers, teachers are allowing their students to make hypotheses about the nature of language and to test these hypotheses through use.

---

[4] NCTE Commission on Composition, "Teaching Composition: A Position Statement," *College English* (October 1974), pp. 219–220.

chapter **II**

THE WRITING WORKSHOP

In the writing workshop, students and teacher work as nearly like professional writers as possible. They keep journals and write in them regularly. Although the teacher may suggest subjects, students are encouraged to discover their own topics. They write in quantity, keeping individual folders or portfolios of their writings, and revise some writings more extensively than others. Students work in **small** and **large groups,** sharing their work and responding to the writing of their peers. Ideally, grades are not given for individual papers. A contract system for grading may be used, or students may choose and submit a series of papers for evaluation. Writers write in a variety of forms, present their writings to a variety of audiences, and publish in personal and class booklets. They may also submit a final draft to a contest or commercial publication.

THE ENVIRONMENT

The classroom environment of the workshop is one in which student writers feel comfortable and safe, a place where they risk being heard by others, where they interact and share ideas openly without fear of destructive criticism. The ideal writing climate is one in which writers both talk and write because they have something to say and someone to respond to that message. The atmosphere is not competitive but one in which each student works to become a better writer while helping and encouraging others to do the same. There is not just one teacher, but many, because students share in the responsibility of helping one another learn and grow. The desks are frequently arranged in large and small circles for group work. Through group work, students not only learn about self-evaluation but analyze and evaluate the writing of their peers. The writing workshop becomes a laboratory in which students often function at the highest levels of thinking. (See Chapter Four for suggestions for developing such an environment.)

Above all, the workshop approach makes writing satisfying for students.

> I like the things we do in our class. At first, I didn't like the circle at all, but now I do. I used to never talk in front of people. I think the circles help a lot. Every class should do it. I think the class is great!
>
> Kris

I wasn't too sure about this class at first. I thought, "Gosh, I have to read out loud to the class." That was bad enough, but it was to be my own writing. But the more I do it, the easier it gets, and I like it.

Arlin

This class is pretty neat. We learn about each other. That's what makes us a special class. I like how we share stories by sitting in a circle and giving each other ideas and help. I enjoy this because it gives me better ideas about stories I write and how to make them better instead of throwing them away.

Sheila

Traditionally, grades have been used as the primary motivators. The teacher served as both audience and critic. By expanding the writer's audience to the writer's own peer group and beyond and ensuring a genuinely caring atmosphere, you will create a classroom which motivates student writers to write honestly and genuinely, rather than producing teacher-pleasing "correct" papers which carefully say nothing.

THE TEACHER

If teaching writing could be reduced to a specific set of step-by-step skill drills, educators would have agreed long ago on an ideal and uniform approach to the teaching of writing. But as the National Council of Teachers of English discovered when it sought out successful teachers of writing, the issue is much more complex. The NCTE study described the methods of about 40 outstanding teachers, and the conclusion was that everyone's method was different.[1] However, as we have learned more about how writers learn to write, some qualities that are basic to the methods of successful teachers of writing are apparent.

The successful teacher of writing is convinced that writing is at the heart of the language arts curriculum. Not only does the teacher provide compelling arguments for the importance of writing in today's society but he or she is equally convinced that writing enables students to arrive at self-knowledge and self-understanding. This enthusiasm is contagious. As students write, the classroom is structured for success, and students look forward to writing again. The teacher programs for frequent writing (knowing that quantity precedes quality) and enables students to write in a variety of forms, fostering both flexibility and fluency. Most important, the teacher writes along with the students and shares the writing with the class, encouraging their comments and suggestions. The teacher models for the students and demonstrates that writing is a skill which

---

[1] Patricia Geuder, Linda Harvey, Lloyd Denis, and Jack Wages, eds., *They Really Taught Us How to Write* (Urbana, IL: NCTE, 1974).

needs continuous practice. The student audience is as valuable to the teacher's growth as a writer as the teacher is to theirs.

The teacher also values the students and their interests and ideas. Hearing what students write about provides a wonderful opportunity to know and care about them. As one teacher exclaimed, "For the first time as a teacher, I can really make a difference. It's no longer an adversarial system." Students are grateful for the teacher's caring:

> I've really enjoyed your class, and I honestly can say I've learned to like writing. . . . whenever I am doing some good writing, I'll re-member you and this class.

> Todd

Parents, too, appreciate what happens in the writing workshop:

> I would like to thank you for the encouragement you've given my daughter. It has truly given her lots of direction and a goal to strive for. . . . She is thrilled that some of her stories made the school paper. . . . We are proud of her, of course, but to have someone else praise her efforts has built up her self-esteem. . . . It means a lot to a young person to have a teacher who can see the possibilities in them.

> Mrs. Swanson

The teacher values the students and honors the writing coming from their experi-ence. She or he provides stimulus for writing but also encourages them to dis-cover their own topics or choices. Often, students will say, "Nothing has happened to me," but the teacher helps them discover that their lives are filled with experi-ences waiting to become their writing. As Frank Whitehead points out, "The real problem that the teacher of English has to face is not how to supply his pupils with 'matter' to write about; it is rather to develop within the classroom the climate of personal relationships within which it becomes possible for them to write about their concerns which already matter to them intensely."[2]

This is primarily experience-based writing. Besides encouraging free choice of topics, the teacher searches for forms of writing that will be enjoyed, encourages recording of personal thoughts and opinions in journals, lets it be known that questions about technical difficulties are always welcome, and above all, offers generous, genuine praise. A successful writing class is invariably a confidence building class.[3]

---

[2] Frank Whitehead, *Creative Experiment* (London: Chatto and Windus, 1970), p. 85.
[3] R. D. Walshe, "What's Basic to Teaching Writing?" *English Journal* (December 1979), pp. 51–56.

chapter *III*

PREWRITING TECHNIQUES

As researchers have studied successful writers, it has become apparent that prewriting is a significant stage in the writing process. As a result, many classroom teachers have come to use a variety of helpful prewriting techniques: brainstorming, listing, freewriting, marathon writing, visualization, clustering (webbing or mapping), and journal writing. These techniques are intended to help students discover meaningful topics and to begin gathering information prior to the drafting stage of the writing.

BRAINSTORMING

Brainstorming is a useful prewriting technique for generating writing ideas, especially when a class is working on a particular topic. Students have an opportunity to verbalize their own ideas and to hear those of their classmates. Each writer draws from the "pool of ideas" produced by the entire class in a brainstorming session.

As students become more adept at generating their own ideas, the group brainstorming session may be eliminated. At first, however, whole class brainstorming may be necessary to help students develop ideas for writing.

Brainstorming Techniques

1. In the brainstorming session, you serve as facilitator, asking open-ended questions ("What is interesting about this idea?"), listening to students express their ideas, probing for more complete responses, and then asking more open-ended questions. Students offer thoughts and ideas on a particular topic, and the responses of the students build on one another.

2. You make a record of student ideas in no particular order on newsprint or the chalkboard. Record *every* response and avoid value judgments. There is no wrong answer. You may abbreviate the ideas, but do not change them.

Studies dealing with creativity show that when creative people come up with an idea, they do not reject it immediately because of its flaws. They play with it, looking for strengths. Students need practice in brainstorming for a quantity of new ideas while *learning to reserve judgment* for a later time.[1]

---

[1] David Campbell, *Take the Road to Creativity* . . . (Niles, IL: Argus Communications, 1977), pp. 13–23.

Listing

A simple variation of brainstorming is listing. Encourage students to make long lists of ideas about possible topics. Lists may revolve around a common theme (e.g., "List as many of your good writing experiences as you can recall").

1. Once students have completed their lists, ask them to focus on a particular item on the list which interests them and add still more ideas (e.g., "Pick one item and list as many details as possible").

2. After students have completed their lists, have them work in pairs, taking turns discussing their ideas and clarifying the plan each has for a writing. (Rehearsing)

3. After the pairs have completed their discussion, have them return to the larger writing group to explain the ideas they've gathered and to describe their plans for a potential draft. Group conferences such as this help writers to focus their purpose for writing.

Freewriting

Freewriting (also known as "sprint writing" or "rush writing") is an excellent prewriting technique for discovering ideas. (It may also be used for drafting.) The writer begins by putting down whatever comes to mind. The temptation is to pause, reread, and edit along the way, but the writer keeps the pen or pencil moving forward, capturing as many ideas as possible. As the ideas come quickly, sentences may become fragments or single words. If the spelling of a word is uncertain, the writer uses it anyway. There will be time in a later stage of writing for checking spelling and for revision to more coherent sentences and paragraphs. It helps if you demonstrate this on the board and freewrite along with your class.

The goal at this stage is quantity of ideas. If the writer runs out of ideas, she or he may repeat the last words written or write over and over "I have nothing to write" until new ideas come, and they do.[2] The first freewritings may be timed for from three to five minutes. You'll need to encourage students first learning this technique to write for the entire length of time. Provide plenty of practice with this technique and gradually include longer periods of writing on more focused topics.

Freewriting leads to honest writing. A student, putting down words quickly, uses his or her own natural language without pretension. Sometimes writers, after long periods of pencil chewing and gazing out the window, say, "I just can't think of anything to write." Freewriting encourages these students to begin writing anyway, to get their pencils moving across the paper, because ideas will come. This student's freewriting is a good example:

> So far I have nothing to write about—nothing to say—nothing to do
> but sit here and think about what I can write about—I'm about at

---

[2] Peter Elbow, *Writing with Power* (New York: Oxford University Press, 1981), pp. 13–19.

the end of my hope with writing without repeating myself. My parents have a positive attitude. In seventh grade I got a "D" on my report card in social studies. This really was hard on me because there was more competition here than in the little country school. I went home with my report card and showed it to my parents when I thought they were in a good mood. I hit it lucky. At the table after everyone was finished I said, "I got my report card and you won't like it.". . .

The student has found a topic! Most of the introductory material will later be discarded, but the early freewriting was necessary in helping her discover what she had to say.

Marathon Writing

Marathon writing is a variation of freewriting which is useful, when all else fails, in helping a class generate ideas. It is conducted in the following manner:

1. Assign students to three groups.
2. Ask each student to jot down three possible writing topics on separate sheets of scrap paper. Collect the slips and place them in a single container. (At this point approximately 75 writing ideas may have been generated.)
3. Draw three slips of paper from the collection and read the suggested topics to the entire class.
4. Instruct everyone in the class to freewrite for a prescribed amount of time (four minutes works well) on one of the three selected topics or on any other topic of their own choosing. (They may, for example, write about an idea they had earlier submitted on one of their own slips of paper.)
5. After the writing time has elapsed, ask the members of one group to read their freewritings aloud. (The decision as to which group reads first may also be made by a drawing.) Give the students in this group a few minutes to edit before they read. They may decline to read if they wish, although the goal is to encourage every student to read at least once in a complete marathon session.
6. Draw three new topics from the container and read these aloud to everyone.
7. Direct all students to freewrite again for another four minutes. They may continue their original freewriting, respond to someone else's writing, write on one of the three new topics, or pick a topic of their own.
8. After the second writing time has elapsed, call on a second group of students to read aloud.
9. Following the reading by the second group of students, draw three new topics from the container and read these aloud. Once again, students may

continue working on an earlier topic, choose one of the newly announced topics or write on a topic of their choice. Some students may choose to focus on a single idea throughout the exercise.

10. Finally, after the third drafting time has elapsed, call on the last group of students to read aloud. Invite any students who have not read previously or any who would like to read again, to do so.

Marathon writing is an enjoyable group activity that generates many, many writing ideas and also allows students to benefit from and respond to the writing ideas of others in the group. Topics discovered in this way undergo further revising and editing during later class periods.

Visualization (Time Travel or Guided Imagery)

Visualization encourages students to travel mentally to another time or place, to an imaginary locale or to a real memory from their past. It is an exercise which often helps writers to generate more specific details and a wider range of sensory description. The following is a sample direction:

> Close your eyes and relax your body. Make yourself as comfortable as possible. We are going on a trip together. You are walking along a path. Look at it carefully. What do you see? What do you smell? At the end of the path is a building. What does it look like? How do you feel? You enter the building. Look at the first room carefully. What are the details of this room? Examine them carefully. Across the room, you see an object which fascinates you. You walk to it, pick it up, and examine it. You carry it from the room and walk back along the path. Returning home, you set the object on your desk and continue to look at it carefully. When you have examined it completely and are ready to write, pick up your pen or pencil and freewrite a description of the object you have discovered on your travels.

After the drafting is completed, students enjoy sharing their writings aloud and comparing their "discovered" objects with other students. You may create an endless number of new circumstances in which to use this kind of lesson. For example, if you want to have students describe a place or event, you might invent a visualization exercise which focuses on a mental trip to a childhood home or to a memory or to a favorite place. Questions such as "What do you see? What do you hear? What can you smell?" are part of the visualization design and encourage the writer to appeal to all senses in the resulting draft. (See Lesson Twenty-eight in Part Two for such an exercise.)

CLUSTERING (MAPPING OR WEBBING)

Clustering is an ideal prewriting activity. It is a nonlinear brainstorming process that generates ideas, images, and feelings around a stimulus word. It works because it seems to avoid critical censorship and allows students to make intuitive connections. A cluster may be expanded endlessly. Encircled words radiate outward, leading writers to sudden ideas and connections that become potential ideas for writing. See the sample:

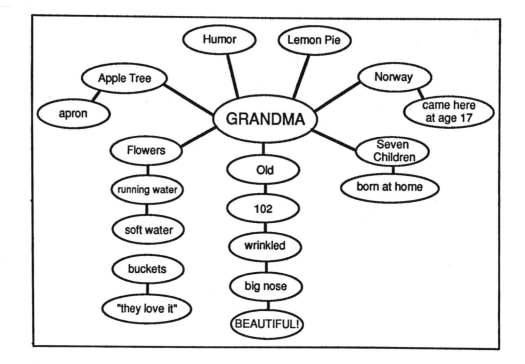

Steps in Learning to Cluster:

1. Explain to the students they are going to learn to use a tool, similar to brainstorming, which will also enable them to discover and explore new writing ideas.

2. Encircle a word on the blackboard, for example, the word "afraid," and ask, "What do you think of when you see this word?" Write down all the student responses (radiating outward).

3. When the students have finished giving their responses, point out, "See how many ideas we have discovered. If you cluster on your own, you will have your own set of unique connections."

4. Ask students to cluster independently. They may begin with a nucleus word of their own or use suggested words such as "help" or "part." Encourage students to cluster for several minutes or as long as necessary. When they *feel* they have arrived at a point where they see ideas and connections, they may begin drafting. Gabriele Rico encourages writers to con-

tinue clustering until they experience a sense of direction, an unmistakable sensation that "you have *this* to write about."[3]

5. Successive clusters can help students narrow a topic that is too general.

JOURNALS

Journals are especially valuable for student writers because they provide a risk-free setting for writing practice and a nonthreatening means for experimenting with and exploring language and ideas. Although read by the teacher, the journal is *never corrected or graded.* Because journals can be read fairly quickly, they allow you to increase the amount of writing students do without increasing your own grading burden.

A journal has many other advantages. It helps to instill writing as a habit and, because of its nonthreatening nature, encourages reluctant writers while allowing good writers the opportunity for experimentation and practice. Journals may also enhance students' self-concepts. The journal is a safe place for them to write about their feelings, their fantasies, their abilities, their limitations, and their views of the world. As each becomes a better observer, formerly unnoticed incidents and facts take on new meaning. The journal can also help establish a sense of continuity in the student's life. Because it is a collection written over a period of time, a writer sees progress, sees ideas develop and change, and arrives at a better self-perspective and self-understanding.

In addition, the journal allows you to know all your students, their likes and dislikes, their backgrounds, and their emotional and social needs. When you read and respond to journal entries, a sense of trust and communication is likely to follow.

Suggestions:

1. Although journals come in all shapes and sizes, a new, standard-size notebook is excellent for journal writing. Encourage students to carry the notebook with them regularly and to use it only for journal writing.

2. Introduce journals after students understand the concept of freewriting.

3. Collect journals at regularly designated times. (Every two weeks is a manageable schedule.)

4. Be sure students clearly understand how a journal differs from a diary. Because diaries are frequently sold with a lock and key, many students believe it is a place for writing secrets. Students need to understand that while a journal is private, it is not meant to be filled with confidences.

---

[3] Gabriele Rico, *Writing the Natural Way* (Los Angeles: J. P. Tarcher, Inc., 1983), pp. 63–87, 90.

However, it is personal, even intimate. There is a very fine line here because freewriting leads to honest, truthful writing, and it is read by at least one other person, the teacher. When the journal is in your possession, take care to see that it is read by no one else. If students wish, they may share entries with others but are never forced to do so. They may, however, want to share a writing because entries are often good and frequently powerful.

This is a very important consideration for every teacher, particularly with laws requiring reporting of suspected abuse. You may occasionally come across a troubling entry, and you will need to decide *before* such an occurrence whether to violate the confidentiality of the journal. Some teachers explain to their students beforehand that if a particular entry makes the teacher fear for their safety, the teacher *has* to do something about it. Troublesome entries are signals of need, and most students who write in such a manner are asking for help and are often willing to consult a counselor or proper agency if encouraged to do so. Ideally, a student's writing should never be used as evidence against him or her.

On the other hand, the journal also encourages experimentation, and every entry need not be "true." One teacher tells about a particular student's journal. The subject matter began to change. New entries focused on stories of drugs and dangerous activities. Naturally, the teacher was concerned and mulled over a proper response. Two weeks later, the journal was submitted again. This time there was a prefatory note: "Don't worry, Mrs. K., those things didn't really happen. It's just that I think my mother has been reading my journal, and I was just trying to find out."

5. You may suggest to students that they fold the page over and/or mark "don't read" alongside entries they consider too personal. Some teachers ask students to mark entries they particularly wish to have read, thus saving time and freeing teachers from reading every entry.

6. Journals are never corrected or graded. Although you may not read each entry, your comments about particularly good entries and interesting ideas are necessary. Sometimes a student and teacher carry on long dialogues in a journal, conversations which may never be mentioned one on one.

7. Initially, journal entries may be practiced in class. However, encourage students to begin the habit of always carrying their journals with them so these are available when a thought occurs or when they want or need to write. In the workshop, journal writing is considered to be primarily an out-of-class activity as a means of encouraging students to observe and to react in writing to *all* their experiences.

8. Students need to understand that *not every entry will be excellent.* A journal is a place for practice. Sometimes the writing will be wonderfully successful; other attempts won't work as well.

9. Occasionally ask students to share a particularly good entry with the class. This is useful if it is not a surprise and if students are asked to read entries they feel comfortable sharing.

10. Ideally, you will also keep a journal and occasionally share your own entries with the class.

11. Structure the class so that students are expected to develop at least one entry into a more polished writing. This is important if students are to see the value the journal has in helping them discover their own topics.

12. After about six weeks, have students evaluate their own journals. If they're writing boring, diary-type entries, they'll often recognize this and change their approach. They'll enjoy the chance to "look back" as well.

Providing for journal writing is one of the most useful writing activities you can design. Handled with care, journals are a safe place for students to practice writing, take risks, and find topics about which they truly care.

chapter IV

RESPONSES

SELF-EVALUATION

Once students have completed a freewriting, they rework and revise it, keeping passages which are good and omitting those which are unnecessary or repetitious. They change the writing in any way they feel necessary to present it to an audience. Over the course of the year, students do become better editors of their own papers because they learn from their own revisions and from the revisions of others. Their proofreading skills are sharpened, and they wish to edit well because they understand they will be sharing their writing with an audience of their peers as well as outside audiences. Student editors may work from checklists such as the following.

A Sample Checklist for Self-Evaluation:

1. Have I reread this paper as if it were a writing I have never seen before?
2. What is the purpose of my paper?
3. Does my writing make sense?
4. Will the reader understand what I wish to say?
5. Have I made all the changes I think necessary?

Individual checklists may be duplicated and distributed to each student or simply written on a blackboard. As the year progresses, additional elements may be added to the checklist as the students are introduced to them.

Will the beginning of my paper "hook" my reader?
Have I substituted specific words for general ones?
Have I appealed to more than one of the five senses?
Have I added similes and metaphors? (These usually have to be added in a second draft.)
Have I removed clichés?
Do I have dialogue, and should I add more?
Have I cut out all unnecessary words? (Words like "and," "then," and "so")
Have I omitted unnecessary adjectives and adverbs?
Have I used good verbs?
Does my writing have a focus?

Do I make my reader see?
Have I corrected any spelling or punctuation errors?
 (This question is reserved for nearly completed
 drafts.)

The Teacher as Responder

As a teacher working with writing as a process you will be involved with students at every stage of the writing, particularly revision. You will want students to understand that revision can lead to discovery and new choices. Ideally, refrain from writing on student papers. If written responses are necessary, comments may be made on removable, self-stick notes attached to the writing. Each teacher has his or her own approach, of course, and if you wish to make comments directly on students' papers remember to balance positive and negative comments.

Student-Teacher Conferences

Conferences can occur at any point in the writing process. They allow writers to get feedback and make improvements as they write. Early conferences between a teacher and student are usually brief and focus on the content of the writing because that is what deserves attention first. Responses such as "tell me about what you are writing" or "how is it going?" are important for early drafts. This is a difficult technique because we are used to pointing out what we think should be done. In this type of conference, you need only restate or summarize what the speaker has said. Your role is to help the student clarify his or her purpose and realize the choices each has as a writer.

Conferences usually focus on one element at a time. A conference might, for example, be devoted entirely to the shape or design of a writing. It might be a discussion of the options the student has for choices of genre or point of view. "What is your plan for telling this story?" is a helpful teacher question in this kind of a conference.

Still other conferences may have to do with the process the student has followed in writing the draft. "Where are you in the writing process?" or "How did you go about this?" are helpful teacher questions. You may also want to discuss the options the writer has for the next step in the writing process. ("What do you plan to do next?")

Conferences should also allow students to evaluate their progress. "Are you pleased with this writing?" "What part do you like best?" "What has caused you the most trouble?" "What have you learned from this writing?" Sometimes questions such as these help a writer decide to revise again.

Later conferences may have to do with editing for mechanical concerns. These are more successful if they do not deal with too many kinds of errors in a single paper. Focus on one particular skill at a time. One approach is to have students proofread their own papers first, then have an editing conference with a classmate, and, finally, confer with the teacher.

Record Keeping

Some teachers keep a set of 5″ by 8″ cards in a file box as a method of recording conferences with students. A separate card is kept for each student and is available to students at any time. As you confer, write a brief summary on the front of the card such as "working on setting—planning to add sensory words." At the next conference, review the card with the student, then go on to discuss the student's progress. You might want to reserve the back of each card to note particular skills being worked on. When one card is filled, staple another to it. At the end of a grading period, the cards provide a good record of the student's progress.

PEER CONFERENCES (THE SMALL CIRCLE)

Peer conferences are a gradually learned process and can occur with one other student, with a small group, or with the entire class. As with student-teacher conferences, peer conferences depend on an atmosphere of mutual trust and respect. (Establishing such an atmosphere is discussed further in the section in this chapter concerning the large circle.) Peer conferences are most likely to succeed after students have seen the process modeled by the teacher in a one-to-one conference with a student or in a whole class demonstration. Several teachers may demonstrate a peer conference for several classes of students at one time, or you may rehearse a small group of students to demonstrate a peer conference for the entire class.[1]

GROUPING

The size of a small group may vary from two to five people and depends upon the number of students you wish to respond to others' papers as well as the amount of time you want to devote to it. A triad offers at least two points of view and requires less time. A group of four or five is large enough to function if someone is unprepared, yet small enough to discuss most pieces of writing in one session.

One advantage of the writing workshop is that while students in a class may have widely differing abilities, *each* can grow as a writer. The class challenges everyone without setting up high levels of frustration. Learning can and does take place for every student. At first, you may assign groups randomly. Later, as you recognize the differing abilities of the students, you may purposely design groups so that each is comprised of high, middle, and low ability students. Some teachers put students together who face similar writing problems. The least desirable approach is to allow students to select the members of their own groups.

---

[1] Donald M. Murray, *A Writer Teaches Writing: A Practical Method of Teaching Composition* (Boston: Houghton Mifflin, 1968), pp. 131–132.

Studies of group dynamics have shown that the productivity of a group increases as the cohesiveness of the group increases. Much of what may appear to an observer as wasted playtime within groups is actually necessary for the group to be productive. When cohesiveness becomes too great, however, productivity declines.[2] With this in mind, encourage a cheerful group atmosphere but change the groupings frequently throughout the year. Be prepared for some chaotic "failed" peer conferences. Working together cooperatively is not a skill most students have necessarily had practice doing. It will take practice and patience and encouragement from you for your students to work well together. Successful peer response groups will evolve over time.

FORMAT FOR RESPONDING

It is important that every response to a writing be made in a positive, constructive manner. Positive reinforcement and honest praise promote learning, whereas an emphasis on errors inhibits it.[3] In their earliest work in the circle, encourage students to point out only *what is good* about a writing. Despite this, many students will rush to point out errors (especially involving mechanics), because they believe that "criticism" means to find fault. They need first to understand that good writing is much more than mechanical correctness, and they need to be encouraged to find examples of strong elements in the writing of their peers. There will be time later to point out weaknesses.

Small-group conferences are usually most successful if they follow a predictable routine or plan. One small-group format which works well is the following:

1. The writer reads his or her paper aloud. (At a later stage of the writing, copies may be duplicated for each group member, but in responding to an early draft, reading aloud focuses attention on ideas and content rather than mechanical correctness.)
2. Each member of the peer group responds as the writer asks the following questions:
   a. What do you like about my writing?
   b. What questions do you have concerning my writing?
   c. What suggestions can you give me for improving my writing?

Encourage authors to take notes at each conference, jotting down ideas and suggestions. Another option is to provide editing sheets for each member to fill out in writing. At the end of a session, the sheets are given to the author and further

---

[2] B. Aubrey Fisher, *Small Group Decision Making: Communication and the Group Process* (New York: McGraw-Hill, 1974), pp. 30–36.
[3] Barak Rosenshine and Norma Furst, "Research on Teacher Performance Criteria," *Research in Teacher Education* (Englewood Cliffs, NJ: Prentice Hall, 1971).

discussion may follow. Written responses are helpful early in the year for some classes, particularly if students have had no previous practice in reacting to the writing of others. Putting their own evaluations in writing helps members of the peer group focus their own thinking.

Encourage students to give specific responses. Rather than saying "I like it a lot," a strong response might be "I like your use of dialogue" or "I like the verb you used in this sentence." Once the writer receives responses and suggestions from his or her peers, each continues to rework and revise. The small circle may reconvene several times to offer additional suggestions and comments. Sometimes students responding to a particular writing have differing suggestions. The student author weighs the opinions of each but makes his or her own final decision about any changes.

As the students work in groups, move among them, observing the interaction and helping when a group has a question. You may take turns becoming a member of each small group, occasionally offering your own writing for consideration. (Don't offer a "perfect paper." Ask the students for their help.)

Students keep early drafts in individual folders and later return to these "portfolios" to choose papers for more extensive revision. Copies of more completely realized revisions are shared in the large circle and are published in class booklets.

The final step in this stage of the process is proofreading for spelling, punctuation, and mechanics. The goal is to make writers *want* to edit well. If students care about their ideas and have good support and peer response, they will want to present their ideas in a neatly written form. If you see common errors, present whole class minilessons which concentrate on one kind of error. The rules of usage are best learned and remembered when they are applied to a writer's own writing. Most of all, encourage an attitude that all writers make mistakes, and all writers need to consult a dictionary, a thesaurus, or an editor.

Working in small groups is more than a useful management technique. Interaction is one of the essential ingredients for learning. In small-group discussions, students explain their viewpoints, validate facts, deal with contradictions, and, at times, change their own attitudes. They become aware of different points of view, rethink their own ideas, and become more objective in their understanding. It is a setting where writers can take risks, where emphasis isn't always on being right but on exploring ideas, where not only is there room for error, but where errors are seen in light of their potential for new understanding.

Additional Guidelines for Small-Group Work

1. Expect each student to share a writing. In the beginning, some teachers allow a reluctant student to pass (not read his or her piece aloud). You might allow students to pass a designated number of times or volunteer to read the piece for the student. Generally, this becomes less of a problem as students become used to reading aloud and if they know at the beginning of a writing that they will be sharing it with others.

2. Encourage students to choose their own topics. No one is forced to read something which may be embarrassing to him or her. Sometimes, however, students do write a paper they later wish not to share. Recognize this possibility. Encourage the student to share his or her next paper when the time comes or to write and present a new piece to the class in its place. This problem is more likely to appear early in the class before students have much experience in the circle. As they learn to expect to share their writing with others and as they come to know and trust one another, they are less likely to have this concern.

3. Some students may write about volatile subjects. As they feel more secure in the class, topics such as personal experience with alcoholism or abuse may emerge. Students who write personally about such topics are dealing with these problems in a healthy way. However, these topics can have an enormous effect on an audience. Other students may feel that unless they, too, write about such subjects, their writing is less valuable. Keep your response in perspective. If you spend an inordinate amount of time responding to inflammatory topics and less time with more ordinary topics, other students will feel the need to write in a confessional mode. No student should feel pressured to do so, but those who need to do so should feel that freedom as well. Balance is important. The writing workshop is not a place for writing about secrets. On the other hand, writers write about honest feelings, and these may include painful topics.

A Sample: Students Responding in the Small Circle

Eric presented the following writing to his group:

> The day was Aug. 12, 1973.
>
> We were headed for Las Vages
>
> "70 degrees on the desert" droned the radio announcer. It was towards evening and the purples, greys, oranges and yellows played across the wild and rocky landscape "Look antilope!"
>
> "get the camera!" "they're to far away." yelled my brother and sister from the back seat. I watched as the antilope leaped out of sight over the hills.
>
> Dad was driving our brown station wagon. Mom and I in the front seat. from the back came the sounds of a game getting underway "geuss what color I'm thinking of!" "Oh, you'll change it when we geuss right" "Oh! Yah!"
>
> "Girls!"
>
> listening to the radio I looked down to the book in my lap, a Trixie Belden mystry

Mom yelled "Look out for that antilope!"

I saw his foot whip to the brake his knuckles turning white on the wheel "Shit."

My eyes traveled from the knuckles to the road, a blur became clear image of the antilope in front of the car. The impact of it hitting the car shook my vision, it was like a lighting bolt had struck at the point of impact. I could see bones and guts coming out of its back. blood splattered across the windshield. the mangled flung itselff in another leaped in front of a camper truck and flipping from it to the ditch in a whirlwind of legs. it lay there eyes glazed and motionless.

Eric

Students found plenty to like about this paper "Oh, it's so gory! But I think it's good gory. I can see what happened." Another said, "I felt like I was sitting in the front seat beside you." Others liked the dialogue. "I can hear the people talking in the car." Another pointed out good verbs like "splattered," and they liked the image in the phrase "a whirlwind of legs." Another said, "I think the paper ends in the right place. It's a good ending."

But the students also had some questions. They wondered exactly how many people were in the car. "Why did somebody say 'Girls'? I thought you mentioned just one sister?" Another pointed out, "I like the dialogue but sometimes I'm not sure who is speaking." Another said, "I wonder if you have to name the book? That sort of distracted me from what happens next." "The word 'shit' bothers me," said another. "Do you think you should use it?" Eric replied, "But that's what he said." "I think it's okay," offered another student. "That's a good way to show he's really upset."

Finally, they made suggestions for making the paper better. "I think you need to think about how the paragraphs are arranged," said one. "Yes," offered another. "Maybe the first three sentences could be in one introductory paragraph?" Later, suggestions were made for getting rid of unnecessary words, and help was given with proofreading. After several revisions, Eric's final version became the following paper:

Vacation in Blood or Gutsy Weekend

The day is August 12, 1973. Our car is headed for Las Vegas.

"Seventy degrees in the desert," drones the radio announcer. It's evening, and the purples, grays, oranges, and yellows play across the wild and rocky landscape.

"Look, antelope!" "Get the camera!" "They're too far away," call my brother and two sisters from the back seat. I watch as the antelope leap out of sight over the hills.

Dad is driving our brown station wagon. Mom and I are the front seat. From the back comes the sound of Janet and Chris playing a game. "Guess what color I'm thinking of."

"Oh, you'll change it when we guess right."

"Oh yeah!"

"Girls!" my dad yells over his shoulder. Country music is playing on the radio, so I begin to read the mystery book on my lap.

"Patrick, look out for that antelope!" Mom yells.

I see Dad's foot jerk to the brake and his knuckles turn white on the steering wheel. "Shit," he says. My eyes travel from his knuckles to the road. A blur becomes a clear image of an antelope. The impact of it hitting the car shakes my vision, and it feels like a lightning bolt has struck us. I can see bones and guts coming out of its back, and blood is spattered across the windshield. The mangled thing flings itself in another leap in front of a camper truck and flips from that to the ditch in a whirlwind of legs.

We all get out of the car and walk to where it is. The eyes are glazed and motionless.

Eric

THE LARGE CIRCLE

When revisions have been polished as completely as possible, ask the students to arrange their desks in a large circle in the classroom to read their papers aloud to everyone in the class.

If students have already had positive experiences in sharing their writing with their peers in small groups, they are likely to continue to do so willingly. However, some students with little confidence and little experience in sharing may be reluctant to do so. Early in the year one student wrote in her journal,

> This class might turn out to be fun. But the bit about reading to other people is a little ridiculous. Some people in here shouldn't hear anything about anyone else. I certainly don't want what I write being blabbed around school.

Sharing papers is a concern for students of all ages. They feel uncertain and insecure and resist exposing their ideas or feelings for fear of ridicule. Indeed, for many, their earlier experiences with writing may have taught them to expect negative criticism and fault finding. They don't willingly enter into an activity that they perceive as threatening. Most classrooms can achieve a reasonable level of trust, but some will not. Don't blame yourself when that happens in spite of your best trust-building efforts.

There are three types of large group activities you might use which are helpful in quickly acquainting the students with one another, setting up an atmosphere of trust within the classroom, and sustaining a supportive atmosphere throughout the year. These are get-acquainted activities, trust exercises, and large circle questions.

Get-Acquainted Activities

At the beginning of the year, it is important for you to learn to know your students and to help them get to know one another as quickly as possible. Many teachers ask pairs of students to interview one another and then introduce their partners to the class. A variation of this activity is to ask students to do the interview and then write a "recipe" for the partner, reading it to the class. (See Lesson Eleven in Part Two of this book for such an activity.)

We often make the assumption that most students in our classrooms know one another. They do not. Even in twelfth grade many students are acquainted only superficially. In a typical class a shy student may sit for months alongside students whose names he doesn't know. Get-acquainted activities are well worth the class time. Writers *need* to know the audience for whom they write, and they need to trust that audience. Listen to one student's comments, for example, concerning his becoming acquainted with others in his writing class.

> This class is so different from all the others that I have ever had. I actually know the people in the class . . . like Laura. . . . She is absolutely beautiful, and I never thought that I would ever be able to talk to her, but this class has made us friends.

> John

Any activity which introduces students to one another and reduces their anxiety is valuable. On some days, as a part of the opening exercise encourage the students to move around the room talking with one another and finding the answers to nonthreatening questions such as

> Who in this class drives the oldest car?
> Who skipped breakfast this morning?
> Whose mother speaks a second language?

(Lesson Twenty-seven in Part Two includes additional ideas for such an activity.)

Trust Exercises

An entire class period spent answering a series of sequenced questions which encourage students to take risks, to respond honestly, and to get positive reinforcement for doing so is helpful for setting a positive class climate. (Lesson Three in Part Two includes such an activity.)[4]

Sometimes the term "trust exercises" is frightening to students. They may approach this type of exercise with some apprehension, and you may choose to refer to it as another get-acquainted exercise. Whatever it is called, it is highly successful in helping students get to know one another quickly. One boy wrote:

---

[4] A book which is helpful for activities such as these is *100 Ways to Enhance Self-concept in the Classroom* by Jack Canfield and Harold C. Wells (Englewood Cliffs, NJ: Prentice Hall, 1976).

At first I was scared. Did "trust exercises" mean we had to do something dumb or give away secrets? But then a pretty girl said she liked my answer. It was neat, and I had fun.

LARGE CIRCLE QUESTIONS

As the year progresses, continue to ask nonthreatening large circle questions. These questions are useful as a means of setting a positive tone in the class, as warm-ups before reading completed writings, as a continued means for students to get to know one another, and as a brainstorming technique for new ideas for writing topics. Ideally, ask two or three questions to begin a class period in which final drafts will be read aloud.

Expect every person in the class to answer each question. It's often helpful if you begin by answering first. If a student doesn't have an answer, continue asking the question around the circle, returning later to those who did not answer. Everyone has equal time to speak. Students will begin to relax and discuss freely. The shy boy who says nothing in a traditional class may turn out to be a clever student with a fascinating hobby. Students look forward to these questions. Many will ask as they enter the classroom, "Do we *get* to have circle questions today?" Invariably when students evaluate the workshop at the end of the year they remark, "The circle questions were fun. I learned so many things about myself and the people in here. I just think we should have done it more often!" With practice, students dare to risk speaking and writing more openly. In addition to becoming better writers, they learn that they are not alone in their teen-age turmoil; that other students share the same feelings, hopes, fears, and uncertainties; and that they have an enormous amount of material to include in their writing. (Notice that the majority of questions suggested in the list evoke positive rather than negative feelings, responses which contribute to a positive atmosphere in the classroom.)

Some Possible Large Circle Questions

1. Describe a simple pleasure in your life.
2. When you were small who were your heroes? Why?
3. What person do you most admire today? Why?
4. Who has been the most influential person in shaping your life?
5. What are the qualities of adults you like most? Least?
6. Tell about your favorite childhood toy.
7. Tell about a time you got in trouble (under age 10).
8. What was the best thing about your neighborhood when you were young?
9. Describe a recurring dream. (Do you dream in color?)
10. Tell about a childhood injury.

11. When you were little did you have a nickname? What was it?

12. Do you like your first name now? If not, what would you choose instead?

13. How would a parent describe you as a child?

14. Describe something you did to tease a brother or sister.

15. How do you feel about school right now?

16. What's the best thing that's happened to you since school started?

17. If you could have one wish come true, what would it be?

18. Name something you hate to do.

19. What is there about you that makes your friends like you?

20. What is the greatest disappointment you have ever had?

21. If your home were on fire, what five things (in addition to your family) would you save?

22. What inscription would you put on your gravestone?

23. What kind of a situation would you like to be in ten years from now?

24. If you could live one day over, what day would you choose? Why?

25. What is a major accomplishment in your life so far?

26. How would your friends have described you in grade school?

27. What is something you've learned in life, so far?

28. In your family, was one child your parent's favorite? How do you know?

29. Have you ever faced death?

30. What is the most humiliating moment you have ever experienced?

31. Do you have trouble with your temper? Explain.

32. Describe the best teacher you ever had.

33. What would the ideal set of parents be like?

34. When you marry someone, do you want that person to be like your father or mother?

35. If this were your birthday and you were your best friend, what would you give yourself?

36. What was the best present or gift you ever received?

37. What is the most humbling experience you've ever had?

38. Describe a time you were pressured to be "in," to be macho.

39. Tell about a time you saw a parent cry.

40. What is the best thing that has happened to you today? In the last week? Over the weekend?

41. If you could teach everybody in the world just one thing—an idea, a skill, a fact—what would it be?

42. If you could be talented in something you are not talented in now, what would it be?

43. Do you have a job now? Describe it.
44. What is the worst job you've ever had?
45. Where were you born?
46. What is your favorite pig-out food?
47. What is your most irrational fear?
48. What is the worst advice your mother or father ever gave you?
49. If you could change one thing about yourself, what would you change?
50. What do you want to teach your own children?

Questions for the End of the Year:

1. Name one thing you've learned about each person in the circle.
2. What mistakes do teachers most commonly make in handling students?
3. If you were principal of this school, what changes would you make?
4. If you were the teacher of this class, what changes would you make?

chapter V

GRADES

As teachers, many of us have evaluated, corrected, and graded student writing in one operation. In the workshop, however, it is useful to make some distinctions between these terms. *Evaluation* is an ongoing process designed to help students be aware of their strengths and weaknesses. It is the description of the writing as well as of the individual growth of the writer. *Correcting* involves pointing out the student's mistakes. *Grading* is assigning a letter or number to represent the quality of the writing. Even though a grade may be based on some objective criteria, teacher judgment usually enters into the process. A grade is final and tells the student nothing about the strengths and weaknesses of the written work.

THE WRITING CONTRACT

Do teachers of the writing workshop need to grade student writing? Ideally, no! Research on the effects of evaluation of writing in the sense of grading and correcting papers consistently underscores two major concerns:

1. Students dislike and sometimes fear writing because of the corrections.
2. Positive comments about a student's writing do more good than do negative comments.[1]

In the workshop, constant positive evaluation is already going on. Students learn self-evaluation, and peer evaluation in the small and large groups is integral to the structure of the writing course. Frequent student-teacher conferences allow the teacher to be aware of the student's ability and growth as a writer. Comments are made in class on papers where and when they most count. The emphasis is on individual growth rather than on competition between students for grades.

Nevertheless, the school system expects us to grade each student's performance periodically. This is necessary primarily as a means of communicating with parents and as a matter of record keeping within the school. How can we reconcile the philosophy of the class with the school system's need for grades? One

---

[1] Wisconsin Writing Project, *A Guide to Evaluating Student Writing* (Madison: University of Wisconsin Press, 1978), p. 4.

of the best solutions is the contract system. Students agree to fulfill certain obligations in order to earn a particular grade. The sample contract included in Lesson Two, Part Two, was designed by students in a writing workshop.

The differences in the grades in this contract primarily reflect the quantity of writing a student chooses to do rather than the quality of his work. However, if care is taken to design small-group work with plenty of time for teacher conferences and revision, the quality of the student writing can also be high. Another advantage is that students who have come to believe they could never earn a "good grade" in a writing class have renewed hope. As one parent pointed out, "Jim has never gotten above a 'C' in English before. He didn't think he could. He's so excited about this class and is working for an 'A.' He even brings his writing home and shows it to us." In a competitive class Jim may not be an "A" student. However, in the workshop, Jim is competing only with himself, and if he chooses to do all the work the contract requires for an "A" grade, his writing will improve markedly, and this is the goal for every student in the class. The contract is fair. Each student knows exactly what he or she must do to earn a particular grade. At the same time, grading is not being used as a means of negative evaluation. The time you will spend in record keeping is far less than the traditional time spent "correcting" papers.

Another option which may be included in the grading contract suggested in Lesson Two is to require students to submit a polished writing as a display piece for a bulletin board or school exhibition. You may also require students to enter a local or national contest or submit a writing for possible publication. Assignments such as these encourage high quality in final drafts, and students enjoy it. *The Market Guide for Young Writers* by Kathy Henderson, published by Shoe Tree Press, Belvidere, NJ, is updated annually and provides a complete description of a wide variety of publications and contests that accept manuscripts from writers age 18 and under.

FINAL COPY STANDARDS

Teachers wishing to include more emphasis on the caliber of editing in the contract itself can include specifications for the quality of final revisions and publications. For high school students the requirement might be: "no spelling errors, no incomplete sentences, and no errors in punctuation." The disadvantage is that the emphasis is again on mechanical correctness rather than quality of thought. In addition, you will have to spend a great amount of time checking for errors. However, as writing labs with computers and word processors become widely available, the ease of correcting, changing, and reproducing polished copies will be such that this standard will be a more reasonable expectation.

PORTFOLIO GRADE

Another acceptable approach for dealing with grades is to have each student submit his or her folder of writings or selected revisions for review by the teacher. This involves much more teacher time, but grades are based on the growth among several writings rather than judging and grading a specific paper.

HOLISTIC GRADING

When a teacher chooses to determine the overall quality of selected writings submitted by the students, holistic grading may be used. Holistic evaluation is a procedure for sorting or ranking written pieces. With this approach, content and form are considered, but the tallying and marking of errors is not required.

In the simplest form, the teacher reads the first paper, then reads the next and decides whether it is better or worse than the first. If it is better, it is placed on the top of the first. If it is worse, it is placed underneath. The scoring or placing occurs quickly, impressionistically. The reader continues until all papers are arranged from most successful to least successful. A grade is assigned after the ordering is completed.

A second approach to holistic grading is to match papers with another piece in a graded series or to score a paper for the prominence of certain features. Again the grading or scoring is done quickly and is usually guided by a scoring guide which describes particular features of writing with high, middle, and low qualities clearly identified.[2] Content, organization, wording, flavor, and mechanics are features frequently identified in scoring papers in this manner.

CHECKLISTS OR GRIDS

The checklist or grid is helpful for a teacher who must grade final revisions. These enable you to read and react quickly to many student papers with consistency and fairness. A checklist reminds both the teacher and student what the important elements are in a particular assignment and allows the student to understand clearly both the strengths and weaknesses of a particular writing. Ideally, the teacher designs a checklist or grid for *each* writing assignment, emphasizing one or two elements at a time rather than identifying every problem. (Students may be asked to number each line of their text before submitting the final draft in order to help the teacher make reference easily.) The checklist is stapled to the student's paper. The following is an example:

---

[2] Paul Diederich, *Measuring Growth in Writing* (Urbana, IL: NCTE, 1974).

Name _____

Hour _____

Writing assignment _____

Content (15) (Comments are line specific, and the teacher
            mentions both strengths and weaknesses.)

1. Does the beginning "hook" the reader?   5 4 3 2 1 0

   (The teacher makes comments here and circles the points the
   student has earned.)

2. Has the writer appealed to more than one   5 4 3 2 1 0
   of the five senses?

   (Teacher comments are made here.)

3. Has the writer made good verb choices?   5 4 3 2 1 0

   (Teacher comments are made here.)

Mechanics (15)
     1. Spelling   5 4 3 2 1 0
     2. Punctuation   5 4 3 2 1 0
     3. Capitalization   5 4 3 2 1 0
Mechanics total (15)   _____

Content total (15)   _____

Grade total (30)   _____

The checklist keeps a balanced emphasis on various elements of good writing. A student may spell poorly, and yet her ideas may be good. The grid prevents the teacher from penalizing the student too severely for a single editing problem. An ideal variation of this assignment is to ask a student to revise a paper after reviewing the comments on the checklist or grid. The final grade reflects the improvement made in the new draft.

GRADING THAT FOSTERS REVISION

Learning Logs

Some teachers have students keep a learning log of their own revision process. This helps the teacher have a better sense of what is happening in the small groups. In a notebook students draw three columns: *Work in Progress, Partner,* and *What We Worked On.* At the end of each session, they record how they used their time. Knowing they will be accountable helps keep students on track. The teacher grades the learning log rather than the actual writing.

Group Grades

Another approach which greatly helps to reduce the paper load is to have one out of every three students complete a writing piece (along with two photocopies). The writer and two student editors work in the small circle to respond to and revise the writing. When a final draft is completed, the teacher grades the paper, and each participant in the group earns the same grade.

Grading, however necessary, must never become confused with teaching. As professionals, we are able to teach best by working closely with our students when they are in the process of composing itself.

chapter VI

SOME ELEMENTS OF GOOD WRITING

In the workshop setting, the teacher and students respond to one another's writings. With practice, students do become more and more skilled in their responses. Initially, however, if students are asked to name some elements of good writing, they usually point to spelling and mechanical correctness. Beyond that, many have no other definition. One of the goals in the workshop, as it progresses, is to help students define and use as many of the elements of good writing as possible.

There are, of course, few hard-and-fast rules that define good writing. Much good writing happens intuitively. It "feels right." As true as this may be, more precise responses are helpful for student writers. The following discussion is included to help identify features which contribute to good writing.

The samples of student writing in this chapter are not meant to suggest that good writing is only personal narrative and only about traumatic or emotional events. However, when students are allowed to choose their own topics and when they feel safe in the classroom and comfortable with their peers, topics about traumatic events may emerge. If this happens, you can be assured the student is dealing with his or her concerns in a healthy way. Don't invite confessional writing, but be aware of the possibility that it may occur. Be honest with your students. If you see they are in danger, they must know you will and are required to seek outside help for them. Initially, young writers will base nearly all of their writing on fact. Only a small amount will come from their imaginations. As they gain experience as writers, they will move to more and more fiction. Allow for and encourage this possibility as well.

GOOD WRITING IS HONEST

Reading student writing has often been sheer drudgery for teachers. Red-marking all those mechanical errors is time consuming, but, more important, the ideas are frequently dull. We have often responded primarily to mechanical correctness, and perhaps students believe that we don't care so much what students write as long as they say it correctly. Consider this student writing. The assignment, teacher imposed, is called a "novel analysis."

> This story is about four children and the young lives they lived. It started out a very normal life for all of them. Chris which was the

eldest of the four, was around twelve when the story began. He liked to read, write poetry, paint and was a very intellengent young man. Then was cathy an average ten year old girl that was very close to her father. Then came cory and carrie which were born when the book first starts.

The paper goes on to retell the story in detail and then the writer concludes:

I enjoyed the book very much. There is two books following this one and I plan on reading then both. They go on to tell of what heppen to them after they escape. And how they eventually get even with their mother for what she put them through.

A teacher responding to this paper marked each mechanical error, gave the student 6 out of a possible 16 points, and graded it "D+." Additional comments were "What an awful sounding book," and "You didn't proofread your paper. Shame on you." The novel analysis, like the traditional book report, is meant to teach writing while encouraging students to read more widely. Instead, the assignment punishes the student for reading and reinforces a feeling of failure as a writer.

This student is attempting to fulfill a teacher-imposed topic. She has little to say although she pretends she does, and the teacher's response does nothing to make the writer want to write again or to show the student how to write more successfully.

In contrast, consider this writing:

One day last March, I was browsing through the library and found myself staring the psychology section in the face. I thought to myself, "Freud, Harris . . . what a bunch of nuts! This psychology stuff is weird!" But just the same, I picked up a couple of these books and paged through them, noticing all kinds of twenty to thirty-letter words I had never heard before. Yuk! And then I picked up a book called *Why We Do What We Do*. I flipped through the pages in that one, expecting to have the same reaction. But this book was written in a normal vocabulary, and it didn't go into such horrible, boring detail. I decided this book might be worth reading, so I checked the book out and spent the next several days reading. It wasn't that weird, either. All of my beliefs about psychology being completely wacko crumbled. It wasn't all that bad. In fact, I was enjoying the book. . . .

The difference between these two papers is much more than mechanical correctness or the ability of the two writers. The second writer is open and honest. The writing is not pretentious. It began as a journal entry and was chosen by the writer for further revision. It has something to say and says it.

No teacher wants empty, phony writing, but it happens in spite of our many good intentions. There is a way out. Students can write openly and freely about topics they choose and care about. The writing workshop enables this to happen.

GOOD WRITING MAKES THE READER SEE

Students in the workshop quickly understand the power of their good writing. They are able to transfer images and ideas from their own minds to those of the audience. But to make the reader "see" an incident, memory, or idea, good advice for a beginning writer is to focus on a specific instance. Many writers tend to summarize or generalize:

> I remember all the great times my brothers, cousins, and I had together. We'd swim, fish, and get in trouble, but we laughed a lot too. . . .

When a student read this in the circle, others suggested he write about one incident. "Let us see *one time*." Others wanted to know the names of the brothers and what specifically it was they did to get in trouble. The student's new draft looked like this:

> It was a crisp, spring day. My brothers, Dave and Ricky, and cousin, Chip, were launching rockets in our yard. Someone suggested, "Hey, wouldn't it be neat if we could launch these out on the lake?"
>
> We gathered up the rockets and set off for the dock, but the boats were gone. "No problem," Dave assured us, "Let's build a raft."
>
> Wow, what a great idea. We were all busy searching for building materials. Two floats from an old boathouse became the base. Rough planks, an old dock section and five feet of rope became the deck. We worked for nearly three hours, and once we were done, our raft was as good as any aircraft carrier. We loaded the rocket gear, a launch pad, a twelve-volt car battery, three rockets, and a handful of engines. It was my job to paddle. We excitedly cast off, and soon we were drifting down the river to the lake.
>
> The rest of the guys were busying themselves up front like a bunch of NASA scientists preparing for a launch, while I sat in back, happily daydreaming.
>
> Suddenly, the raft bucked and a pontoon erupted from under us. Splash! We began to capsize. I plunged into the icy spring water "Help," someone screamed, "I'm gonna drown." The shore was twenty feet away. We were frantic, splashing and screaming.
>
> I couldn't swim too well, so I dog paddled furiously. Then Rick shouted, "Hey, wait a minute. I can stand." Timidly, I stopped beating the water and tried it too. The water barely came past my waist.
>
> Jim

When the writer first concentrates on one incident, he adds good facts naturally. The audience hears the boys speak, sees them "work like NASA scientists," and sees the humor of the situation without the writer having to say it was funny.

Students quickly understand the power of specific detail. A reader sees "a Daisy B B gun" better than "a toy gun" or a "forty-nine Chevy" better than "my car."
Another student wrote:

> There was a very special person in my life, my grandfather. Our relationship was really special. But he's had a stroke now, and he's changed so much it makes me sad.

Again the students in the circle pointed out that they needed to "see" the grandfather. "What did he do?" they asked. "What did he say?" The writer began listing facts, and, as these accumulated, she created a more complete picture:

> I remember sitting on my grandpa's lap listening to stories of his childhood. He told me of horse-driven plows, wood-heated schools, and homemade bread. My grandpa used to run his own flour mill until he became the town electrician. When he looks at the town lights, he says, "I put up most of the lights in this little town." He liked to hunt and fish, and he was good at it. He has a bald eagle, a pelican, a horned owl, squirrels, and stuffed ducks. He built his grandchildren a large, white swing-set in his front yard, and he spent hours in his garage fixing gadgets or making electrical parts. He rarely watched TV except for the daily news or a football game.
>
> My grandpa loved to talk, and he often argued with my dad (who is a Democrat), "Those darn Democrats. I wish they would quit messin' up the government." When my dad made my brothers help with the dishes, he would say, "You boys come and help me. Let the girls do it. That's women's work."
>
> Now my grandfather just sits in his tan chair in front of the TV. He never goes out of the house to walk, fish, or mow the lawn. He had a stroke that paralyzed his left side. His left leg swells and hurts when he walks. He hardly ever talks or fixes electrical gadgets, and he shaves only once a week. My grandmother helps him get dressed and helps him up from his chair. He spends most days sitting in that chair, gazing out the living room window.
>
> Becky

By giving the reader many facts, the student creates a more complete picture of the grandfather. Although she doesn't write that the change in him makes her sad, the audience is able to see that too.

GOOD WRITING BUILDS

Inexperienced writers often "give away" too much information too early in the writing. For example,

> When I was nine I had a bad experience at a resort, or Something I will never forget is when my cat died, or When I was five I really did a stupid thing.

By beginning this way, writers remove all the elements of surprise. When questioned, however, they quickly acknowledge that as a particular day began, they didn't know they were going to do something silly or have a particular experience. As writers, they need to keep some information from the audience until the appropriate time. They need to plan and shape their final drafts. The following is an example of a writing that builds:

Once a week my grandma visited a friend of hers in the nursing home, and most of the time she brought me with her.

Before we got to her friend's room, we had to walk through the cold, air-conditioned sitting room. It had a white tile floor, fluorescent lights, a T.V., and about twenty, fake leather chairs occupied by the same tired, faded people. At the time I was in kindergarten and had been introduced to seating charts. I remember wondering if the old folks had to go by one also.

My grandma always paused to chat with an old woman who sat in the last chair against the wall. I observed the woman from behind my grandma, afraid I would have to shake one of those gnarly hands.

The old woman looked like an old black hen. She had iron-grey hair in short ringlets. Her ice-blue eyes stared from behind black horn-rimmed glasses, and small liver spots dappled her pale skin. She wore dark clothing that covered most of her plump body. A wooden cane rested against the arm of the chair, and from time to time she picked it up and twisted it in her hands. Sometimes she pounded the floor for emphasis. When she talked, her silver teeth sparkled. She looked mean, but when she spoke, her voice sound young and her laugh was pretty. It seemed as if there was a young lady trapped inside.

Through the conversations I listened to, I learned the old woman had many relatives, but they didn't write or visit. The last time she had seen her favorite son was when her dropped her off at the "Almost-Gone Home," as she called the nursing home.

"Don't talk like that, Myrtle," my grandma told her.

"Why not," she replied. "I'm half-dead anyway."

I couldn't understand how a person could be only half dead, and I wondered what it was like. She looked mostly alive to me.

One day, when we walked through the sitting room, I didn't see the old woman in the last chair. An old man who sat nearby looked up at Grandma and reached out a trembling hand. I saw his mouth quiver as he whispered, "She's gone, Alice. The old lady ain't here no more."

My grandma smiled a sad smile. I wasn't sure that meant the old woman was completely dead or had just moved to a new home, but I was too afraid to ask.

Michelle

GOOD WRITING EXPERIMENTS WITH LANGUAGE

Writers make many good word choices naturally. In revision, students work to replace weak verbs with strong ones. They rely on a thesaurus, adding and substituting words to employ the repetition of sounds, personification, and other figures of speech. This student is aware of the sounds of his words:

> I ran through the woods. My gun jangled from the hundreds of B-B's bouncing inside. I was the big hunter stalking his prey. A flock of songbirds flitted through the trees. As I shot at them, they darted from limb to limb. . . .

Notice the noisy words like "jangled" and "B-B's bouncing," the good verbs like "flitted" and "darted."

Another writer personifies the dark to describe her fear as she sits alone in the living room during a storm:

> The wind screams her agony through the fireplace, sending whitish-gray ashes waltzing upon the carpet. I am a perfect ice-maiden, frozen into my stone chair. Even the picture window shudders, afraid of the dark. Rain, joining forces with the dark, sends millions of tiny footsteps hurrying across the ground. The ceiling glitters an evil flicker as the doorknob trembles and rattles. Finally, darkness saunters through in victory.

> Kim

GOOD WRITING OFTEN USES CONTRAST

The student writing about her grandfather, creates a powerful picture by showing the reader what he had been like earlier and what he is like following a stroke. This use of contrast works well. Another student, writing about the funeral of a grandmother uses contrast within a single sentence:

> Grandma's long brown casket with gold trim looked soft and comfortable, but she looked uncomfortable and arranged.

GOOD WRITING IS ECONOMICAL

How many times do we hear the question, "How long do you want this paper to be?" Many of us have answered, "four typed pages" or "five hundred words"? Students with nothing to say but an assignment to fulfill produce the length the teacher desires. The result is filler. Students may actually spend more time counting words than they spend writing. "This story is about four children," would have been sufficient, but the student, uncertain and concerned with sounding knowledgeable, adds "and the young lives they lived." By adding this kind of filler, she at least achieves the length requirement of the assignment.

The following sample is a paragraph from another student writing. Later the student explained, "Oh, I don't believe all that stuff in my paper, but I know that's what the teacher wants, so that's what I write."

> The author's philosophies of success are almost identical to my own. Because I have always been a success-oriented person, most of his ideas are not all new to me. The way I will reach my success is basically the same as his steps for success. Not only have his steps reinforced my own plans, they have also stressed the importance of dedication needed to attain success.

"Success" is mentioned five times in this paragraph alone. The student, wise enough to know this concept is a high priority with his teacher, uses it deliberately. Had the student been expected to share the writing with a peer group, the unnecessary repetition would have been pointed out. In all likelihood, the student wouldn't have chosen the topic in the first place.

GOOD WRITING FREQUENTLY INCLUDES STRONG REPETITION

Students, writing freely, often use strong repetition naturally. This student uses it for emphasis:

> Last week my Uncle Richie phoned my mom and said, "Grandma is sick and getting worse." He explained that one night he went to pick her up for church and found her sitting in her rocking chair holding her crucifix. She hadn't gotten dressed and didn't have the energy to get up. Mom is going to New York soon to see Grandma. She said I could go along since I am Grandma's favorite grandchild, and there might not be another chance to see her. *But I am not going. I am not going* because Grandma's tickets for me last year and all our good times and talks were her way of saying good-bye to me. That's how I want to remember her, a short plump woman standing in the airport, pressed up against the window, waving both arms, crying, and saying over and over, *"I love you. I love you."*

> Tracy

GOOD WRITING AFFECTS THE AUDIENCE

Strong writing causes something to happen for the audience. It may simply be recognition of a like experience. It may be laughter, a lump in the throat, or a nod of agreement. The following writing, though filled with mechanical errors, is powerful writing:

I followed my mother into the intensive care ward. "Honey were here" she said in a low voice. A maching one of many next to my fathers bed starting beeping faster and slowly he open his eyes. Moms eyes were filled with tears but she managed a half smile and siad "Hi". The maching beeped faster and in a scratchy, dry voice he said "Hello". It became harder and harder to look at him. My father someone I always thought of as strong and stubborn could barely even talk. After seeing him that helpless all I could do was cry. I walked to the window so he wouldn't see me. It was a beautiful day. People walked in the street below and cars went by. The world certainly hadn't stopped for my father or even slowed any. I looked behind me. Tears ran down my moms face as she talked with dad. "Yes dear" "Were in a hotel" "No dear." I just turned an stared out the window. Out in the street people huried back and forth to work or to some important activity. They didn't know my father was dying. They probably didn't care. I wished I was one of those people. His skin was pale yellow and so were his eyes. I felt like I was going to burst from holding back the tears. Luckily my mom said we had to go. As we left the beeping maching slowed and my dad slept. The next day my sister arrived and convinced my mother to take a room at a nearby hotel. We checked in and arrived back at the hospital just in time to hear a page "Colleen Brown please come to the intensive care unit." My mom cried all the way up the elevator. It seemed to take forever to go up three floors. When we got there the doctor explained they had done everything they could. My mother and sister and I all cried. We cried for a long time.

                                                                    Brad

This writing is in desperate need of polishing. It needs commas and paragraph divisions. It is frequently unnecessarily wordy. However, in every other respect, it is excellent writing. The boy writes honestly about his feelings and fears. "I felt like I was going to burst from holding back the tears." He admits he wished he could be somewhere else. He contrasts the father's dying with the happy activity on the street below the hospital window. The reader stands in the room with the boy and "sees." We hear the sounds of the life-support machines and the voices of people speaking. From the beginning of the writing, we know the father is exceptionally ill. Yet the story continues to build. The family rides the elevator to the third floor to hear the doctor's prognosis. And finally, the writing ends with the wonderfully painful repetition, "We cried for a long time." The audience hearing this paper is enormously affected by it.

Students do have something to say, and they can write powerfully. If Brad's paper had been handled in a traditional way, what would have been the teacher's response? Is it a "C" paper, a "D" paper, or should it be marked "F" because of the large number of mechanical errors? In reality the student did polish and revise the paper further, and it was immensely satisfying both to him and his writing circle. Because he cared so completely about his topic and because so many fine elements in his writing were pointed out to him, he wanted to polish it, to add commas and paragraph indention for clarity. He felt like a successful writer and he was. Every student can be.

part two

STEP-BY-STEP WRITING LESSONS FOR THE CLASSROOM

unit 1

BECOMING ACQUAINTED WITH THE WRITING PROCESS

Lessons One through Fifteen in this unit introduce students to the writing process and to concepts such as brainstorming, listing, rehearsing, freewriting, and showing. The writers complete six freewritings and choose one to revise and share aloud with their classmates. *Unless otherwise noted,* each lesson is intended to take approximately one class period. However, because of the nature of writing and the writing process, it may be necessary for you to adjust the time lines to allow for the needs of your own students. Each unit results in a polished writing and requires students to complete the entire writing process.

Classroom Management: Some teachers have been hesitant to introduce the writing process into their classrooms because students often work independently or in small groups, and such classrooms frequently appear to be noisy and active. How can a teacher introduce the writing process and, at the same time, create and administer an environment where students are on task and actively engaged in learning? It does take practice and patience and encouragement on the part of the teacher for students to learn to work cooperatively, but it is a skill which *can* be learned and is satisfying to both students and teachers. Practical ideas to help you create and maintain such a classroom are included throughout the following lessons.

LESSON ONE: INTRODUCTION

Objectives: The students will be able to

- Express their expectations for a writing class.
- Distinguish between the old approach to the teaching of writing and the new.
- Define "freewriting."
- Write an unfocused Freewriting 1.

Procedure:

   I. Introduce yourself and all class members by name.
     Introductory questions:
      A. Why are you taking this class? (Many will say, "It's required." Praise their honesty.)
      B. What do you want to learn?
      C. Why do people need to know how to write?
      D. What is good writing? (Many students will respond with statements about mechanical correctness. Explain that aside from mechanical correctness, there are other elements of good writing. One objective of this class is to help writers discover their own definition of "good writing.")
  II. Discuss the traditional approach to the teaching of writing.
      A. Graded papers
      B. Emphasis on correctness and correcting (a negative process)
      C. Teacher as only critic and audience
 III. Explain the writing process approach to the teaching of writing. (See Part One, Chapter One, for an explanation of all these.)
      A. Prewriting
      B. Drafting
      C. Revising
      D. Presenting or publishing
 IV. Explain additional elements.
      A. Journals (see Part One, Chapter Three)
      B. Topics
        1. Students' choices
        2. Students' experiences
      C. Group work (sharing)
        1. Small circle (see Part One, Chapter Four.)
        2. Large circle (see Part One, Chapter Four.)
      D. Publication
        1. Private booklets
        2. Class booklets
        3. Other audiences (contests, adults outside school, newspapers and other publications, for example)

     E. Grading (see Part One, Chapter Four, for an explanation of the grading contract and other options for evaluation)

  V. Explain what you expect of each class member. For example,

     A. Attend class regularly.

     B. Compete only with yourself to become a better writer.

     C. Work cooperatively in groups.

     D. Share writings in the circles.

     E. Help others to become better writers.

  VI. Explain your classroom management style. (See note at end of this lesson.)

 VII. Introduce *Freewriting 1*. (See Part One, Chapter Three.)

     A. A sample explanation:

> I'm going to ask you to write freely for five minutes. During that time you are to keep your pen or pencil moving forward, and although you will be tempted, try not to stop and reread what you have written. Write about whatever comes to mind. Don't worry about neatness or spelling or punctuation. Capture as many ideas as possible. If you find an interesting idea write about that. If another interesting idea comes along, follow it. Let your writing flow wherever your mind leads. If you cannot think of anything to write, simply write over and over, "I can't think of anything to write," until another idea comes along, and it will.

     B. Students write for five minutes about any topic. Ideally, you will write along with the students.

     C. Discuss

       1. How did it feel to write in this manner? Some possible answers will be:

> "It was hard to keep going."
> "I didn't know what to write about."
> "My arm got tired."
> "It was hard not to reread."

       2. Assure students these reactions are natural. As with any skill, freewriting requires practice, but it is an excellent way for writers to discover writing ideas and topics.

       3. Read your own freewriting aloud, partly to demonstrate how rough a first draft can be.

       4. Collect student Freewriting 1.

If class time allows, you may want to begin helping students arrive at their own definition of "good writing" by studying together the accompanying student writing, *"My Brothers Are Going as Pirates."* Ask the students to point out its strong elements.

Classroom Management: Spend time planning the classroom environment before students arrive in the fall. How will you manage small and large circle arrangements, for example? Students should know where writing materials are kept and what is available for their use. Writers use a variety of utensils, materials, and equipment: different kinds of pens, pencils, markers, paper in a variety of sizes and colors, stationery and envelopes, staplers, staples, staple removers, tape, glue or paste, scissors, erasers, and correction fluid. Must students provide their own equipment, or will it also be available to them in the classroom? Where are the dictionaries and thesauruses? May students check out copies for their use outside of class? What is the procedure? Will student portfolios be kept in the classroom? Where? May students remove the portfolios from the room? Be clear about your expectations and management style. Give students as many responsibilities as possible. Enable them to go about their business of being writers without interrupting you with unnecessary, time-consuming questions such as "May I borrow a pencil?" The goal is to make this a self-starting classroom, a classroom filled with students who come into the classroom and begin work immediately.

Hint for makeup work: Each day on a dated 3″ by 5″ card, write a brief summary of the day's lesson. (Students may be assigned this task.) Make particular note of any writing activity or other assignment and place the card in a holder available to students. When absent students return, they quickly learn the efficient habit of checking these cards for makeup assignments.

1.1 Writing Sample

MY BROTHERS ARE GOING AS PIRATES

I remember a Halloween night. I am standing on top of our kitchen table, and Mom is standing in front of me, hurriedly patting makeup on my face.

"But I don't want to go as a clown, Mom," I complain.

She sighs, "There's nothing else for you to be. Now just be still. It's almost time to go."

The world becomes blurry, and I whine, "You're hurting me."

"Be still," she grumbles, tiredly. "I'm almost finished. There. I'm done. Now that wasn't so bad was it?" She smiles and hands me a mirror.

I look into it sadly. A clown stares back at me, a clown with a white face, red-lipstick cheeks and nose, blue circled eyes, and an ear-to-ear smile. I see a happy clown, but I don't want to be a dumb ol' clown.

My brothers are going as pirates. Greg's wearing a black top hat and sleeveless jean jacket. Garry has on Mom's earrings, a red scarf tied around his forehead, a patch over his left eye, and black jeans. They both have cardboard swords. I don't have a sword. I'm only wearing a tie-dyed t-shirt. I'm just a clown.

I hear my brothers laughing and playing pirate games. Finally, Dad calls, "Let's go." My brothers race to the car and sit on the edge of the back seat, waiting. I get in too, but I don't say anything. When Dad stops the car, my brothers rush to a house and clatter up the steps calling, "Trick or treat." I follow slowly.

A man opens the door. He hold bags of candy and looks at us carefully. Then he laughs as his glance falls on me. "You're the best looking clown I've seen in a long time." I shyly smile a smile equal to the one already on my face. We thank him, and I race to beat my brothers to the next house.

Cindi

LESSON TWO: GRADING CONTRACTS AND WRITING FOLDERS

Objectives: The students will be able to

- Understand what is required to earn a particular class grade.
- Choose the grade they wish to work for and contract with the teacher for that grade.

Procedure:

If you plan to use a contract for grading, follow these suggestions. If not, explain your grading policy. (See Part One, Chapter Four, for a discussion of possible options.)

    I. Distribute the **Grading Contract for the Writing Workshop.**
        A. Hand out copies of the accompanying grading contract to each student.
        B. Answer all questions about the grading system.
   II. Ask students to sign the contract.
        A. Students choose the grade for which they wish to work.
        B. Students fill in the contract, sign it, and return the signed portion to the teacher.
 III. Have students assemble their portfolios.
        A. Hand out a file folder to each student. If these are not available, students can make their own by taping together two sheets of heavy, colored paper.
        B. If you plan to have students do all or most of the writing called for in this book, distribute the accompanying **Checklist for Freewritings and Revisions**. If not, you may wish to design a checklist of your own. Have students secure the sheets in their folders.
        C. Return Freewriting 1 to the students to place in their folders.
        D. Collect the folders or have students place them in the designated location in the classroom.

If there is extra time, point out books in the classroom which students may enjoy reading. Include samples of student writing displayed around the room. This, of course, is important because writers are readers. (Two books which contain writing similar to the writing students are being asked to do in this class are Russell Baker's *Growing Up* and Ray Bradbury's *Dandelion Wine*.)

From time to time, read excerpts from writings you particularly cherish, and be sure to include writing by students as well as professional writers. Also encourage students to find and bring their own samples to class, and take time to read them aloud. Invite professional writers from your community into the classroom as speakers.

TWO SUGGESTIONS:

1. Occasionally ask students to write a memo to you, explaining how well they feel they are meeting the requirements of the contract. It may also be necessary for you to distribute reminders such as the following:

Date _____

Class _____

Name _____

According to my records, you have not completed the

following assignments:

If class grades were to be assigned *today*, your grade would

be _____ .

---

2. The contract that accompanies this lesson requires students to do extra writings for both the A and B contract. You may want to consider the following variations of this requirement:

   a. Have students polish a writing as completely as possible and enter it in a contest.

   b. Have students prepare an illustrated, completely revised display piece for a bulletin board or school exhibition.

   c. Have students submit a final draft for possible publication. The *Market Guide for Young Writers* by Kathy Henderson, published by Shoe Tree Press, Box 219, Crozet, VA 22932, is updated annually and provides a complete description of a wide variety of publications which accept manuscripts from writers age 18 and under.

Name _____ Date _____

1.2 Grading Contract for the Writing Workshop

The writing workshop is based on the philosophy that everyone can be a writer; that is, every student in this class can effectively communicate in writing. In this workshop, you will learn to improve your communication abilities, both written and oral. If you actively participate in the class, you will learn the techniques of good writing, and you will grow as a writer.

This class requires work and commitment from you. You will be asked to write nearly every day. You will read and share your writing with other class members and publish your writing in personal and class booklets. You will help one another become better writers.

Students are expected to earn "A" or "B" grades. You can do this by completing all assignments when they are due, by making a sincere effort to improve as a writer, and by actively participating in the class.

To earn an "**A**," the student does the following:

- ☐ Completes all assigned writing and revisions.
- ☐ Submits a revised writing for each publication.
- ☐ Writes four journal entries per week.
- ☐ Participates actively in both large and small circles.
- ☐ Turns in all assignments, journals, and revisions on or before the due date.
- ☐ Submits two additional writings each quarter, conferring individually with the teacher to carry each writing through the entire writing process.

To earn a "**B**," the student does the following:

- ☐ Completes all assigned writing and revisions.
- ☐ Submits a revised writing for each publication.
- ☐ Writes three journal entries per week.
- ☐ Participates in the large and small circles.
- ☐ Turns in all assignments, journals, and revisions on the due date.
- ☐ Completes one additional writing each quarter, conferring independently with the teacher to take the writing through the entire writing process.

To earn a "**C**," the student does the following:

- ☐ Completes all assigned writing and revisions.
- ☐ Submits a revised writing for each publication.
- ☐ Writes two journal entries per week.
- ☐ Participates only occasionally in the large and small circles.
- ☐ Occasionally turns in assignments, journals, and revisions after the date due.

To earn a "**D**," the student does the following:

- ☐ Completes all assigned writing and revisions.
- ☐ Submits a revised writing for each publication.
- ☐ Writes one journal entry per week.
- ☐ Seldom participates in the large and small circles.
- ☐ Presents work in a sloppy and uncaring manner.

Name _____ Date _____

Grading Contract for the Writing Workshop

I, _____ , understand that in order to
   (name)

contract for the grade of _____ I must and will do the

following:

Date _____

Signature _____

Name _____   Date _____

1.3 Checklist for Freewritings and Revisions

UNIT ONE
Freewriting 1 _____
Freewriting 2 _____
Freewriting 3 _____
Freewriting 4 _____
Freewriting 5 _____
Freewriting 6 _____

Revision 1 _____

UNIT TWO
Freewriting 7 _____
Freewriting 8 _____

Revision 2 _____

UNIT THREE
Freewriting 9 _____
Freewriting 10 _____
Freewriting 11 _____

Revision 3 _____

UNIT FOUR
Freewriting 12 _____

Revision 4 _____

UNIT FIVE
Freewriting 13 _____

Revision 5 _____

Super Revision 6 _____

UNIT SIX
Freewriting 14 _____
Freewriting 15 _____
Freewriting 16 _____
Freewriting 17 _____
Freewriting 18 _____

Revision 7 _____

UNIT EIGHT
Poem 1 _____
Poem 2 _____
Poem 3 _____
Poem 4 _____
Poem 5 _____
Poem 6 _____
Poem 7 _____
Poem 8 _____
Poem 9 _____
Poem 10 _____
Poem 11 _____
Poem 12 _____

Poetry Book _____

UNIT NINE
Freewriting 19 _____
Freewriting 20 _____

Revision 8 _____

Freewriting 21 _____
Freewriting 22 _____

Revision 9 _____

Freewriting 23 _____

Revision 10 _____

Personal Book _____

LESSON THREE: GETTING ACQUAINTED

Objectives: The students will be able to

- Become better acquainted.
- Feel more at ease speaking in the large circle.
- Respond in Freewriting 2 to the get-acquainted activity.

Procedure:

I. Introduce a get-acquainted activity.
   A. Formerly, students wrote only for the teacher.
   B. In the writing workshop, the entire class is the audience.
   C. To write freely and honestly, the writer needs to know the audience.
   D. Although many of the students in the class may be acquainted, there are effective activities for developing understanding and trust.

II. Follow these steps in a get-acquainted, trust exercise.
   A. Seat the group in a large circle. The group leader (you) participates as well and answers first. (Note: Any group members may elect to "pass" temporarily on any question. Come back to them when all others have answered.)
   B. Ask each person to give his or her first name. The students take turns repeating the names of every person in the circle.
   C. Ask each person in turn, "If you were a color, what color would you be and why?"
   D. Ask each person, "If you were an animal, what animal would you be and why?"
   E. Ask each person to introduce himself or herself to the group as if he or she were someone else and have that person say something about him or her. ("Hi, I'm Gertrude. This is my son Tom. He's . . . .")
   F. Ask each person, "What is one thing of which you are proud?"
   G. Ask each person in the group to choose one other person's response to the preceding question and tell that person why he or she especially liked that response. Make sure members address each other directly by name. "Peter, I liked your answer because . . . ." Don't allow a response such as, "I liked Peter's response because . . . ."
   H. If time is limited, stop here. (You'll want the students to respond in writing to this exercise.) It's good to end on a positive note. If there is plenty of time, continue on.
   I. Ask each person, "If you could change one thing about yourself, what would you change and why?"

   J. Repeat activity "G" in response to question "I."
 III. Introduce Freewriting 2.
    A. After the exercise and five to six minutes before the class period is over, ask students to do Freewriting 2.
    B. A sample direction:

     In a freewriting, please respond to the activity we just completed. How do you feel about it? What did you like? What did you dislike? What did you learn?

    C. Collect the responses.

A suggestion: You may want to keep a variety of word games at hand in case the class finishes its work before the end of a period. For example,

Behavior Mod: Two people leave the room. While they are gone, the class decides upon a physical shape or configuration it wants the students to assume. The two reenter the classroom and begin miming a variety of stances. The class claps to signal its desires until the two students are in the shape the class had envisioned.

Mime Rhyme: A student thinks of a particular word and says, "I'm thinking of a word that rhymes with _____ ." People mime words as guesses to the answer.

Remember the old *knock-knock jokes*? Here are a few: Isadore—locked, Sam, and Janet—evening, and Tarzan—stripes forever. Ask the students to invent more.

An excellent source for word games is Herbert Kohl's *A Book of Puzzlements* (New York: Shocken Books, 1981).

LESSON FOUR: WRITING RITUALS

Objectives: The students will be able to

- Review the goals of the class.
- Practice listing.
- Write a ten-minute Freewriting 3, focusing on an early writing experience.
- Understand that most writers have had both good and bad writing experiences.

Procedure:

I. Review some of the goals of the class.
   A. Students will overcome their suspicions of writing.
   B. Students will be freed to express honest feelings.
   C. Students will be encouraged to write about what they know best.
   D. Students will share and publish writings for a variety of audiences.

II. Explain that writers sometimes have "rituals" or preferences that, they believe, help them to write better. Such rituals may have to do with the time of day a writer believes he or she writes best, the kind of pen, pencil, and paper he or she chooses, or the location and the surroundings he or she prefers.
   A. Ask students to list their own writing rituals. (This is good practice in listing.)
   B. Call on every student and ask each to read his or her list. (This is an early, nonthreatening practice in reading aloud.)

III. **PREWRITING:** Introduce Freewriting 3.
   A. Explain that students have had a variety of writing experiences.
   B. Writing has sometimes been used as a punishment.
   C. Some students may not enjoy writing because they feel they do not write well or have had unpleasant experiences.
   D. Many students enjoy writing and look forward to writing again.
   E. Ask the students to make two headings at the top of their papers. "Good Writing Experiences" and "Bad Writing Experiences."
   F. Have your students list in each category as many instances from their own experience as they can recall.
   G. Modeling: Display your own list for the students. Tell the class what you are going to write about and explain why you chose this topic and eliminated the others.

IV. **DRAFTING** *Freewriting 3:*
   A. A sample direction:

Choose one of the ideas on your list. Write freely for ten minutes about a writing experience you have had. Try to focus on one memory. Don't stop to reread or edit. Remember, a first draft should be sloppy, should pay little attention to spelling or punctuation, and should contain no erasures. Let your freewriting help you discover new details in the memory. If you finish before the other writers, wait quietly or reread what you have written and make any changes necessary for clarity. When everyone is ready, we will read these drafts aloud to one another.

    B. Write with the students.

V. **REVISING:** Ask students to edit their freewritings quickly, making any changes necessary in order to read them aloud to the class.

VI. **PRESENTING:**

    A. Each person reads his or her writing to the class. You may wish to model a response, by reading your writing first. Don't rearrange the desks for this exercise. This is an early, low-key practice in sharing aloud.

    B. You may feel this sort of activity takes too much time. Don't trust that feeling.

If there is additional time:

    A. Analyze the components that make a good or bad writing experience.

    B. Reinforce the idea that many students have had both good and bad experiences with writing, but a goal of this writing workshop is to help students overcome negative feelings and to ensure success for every writer.

LESSON FIVE: BRAINSTORMING

Objectives: The students will be able to

- Practice brainstorming and listing as a prewriting activity.
- Do a collaborative group writing.

Procedure:

   I. Explain brainstorming. (See Part One, Chapter Three.)
       A. Brainstorming is a prewriting technique intended to generate many ideas.
       B. Someone makes a record of all the ideas which are generated.
       C. No ideas are ever rejected and discussion is withheld until a later time.

  II. Ask the students to practice brainstorming in groups.
       A. Distribute similar objects to each student. Mini-Tootsie Rolls are ideal (because they can be eaten). Coins, pencils, or other classroom objects are also good options.
       B. Arrange the class into small groups of three or four students each. (Having students number off is an efficient way to manage this step quickly.)
       C. Give each group a large sheet of newsprint. (The large size encourages many responses.)
       D. Have each group pick a student to record ideas.
       E. Ask students to list on the paper as many ideas about their object as they possibly can. You may wish to set a time limit of ten minutes and encourage the groups to compete with one another for the longest list.
       F. When the time is up, have the recorders count the number of ideas each group has listed. (You may want to reward the group having the longest list with additional Tootsie Rolls.)
       G. Have someone from the winning group read its list.
       H. Ask students from the other groups to suggest additional items the first group may have overlooked.
       I. Point out that cooperative brainstorming has allowed them to generate many, many ideas and is a useful technique for every writer.

 III. **DRAFTING:** Explain that each group is to collaborate in writing a description of their object. If you wish, set a time limit of ten to fifteen minutes. A sample direction:

> I want you to continue working in your groups. As a group, write a description of your Tootsie Roll (or coin, or pencil, etc.). Decide beforehand what your approach will be. You may be as

creative as you wish, but remember, the purpose of your writing is to produce as complete a description as possible.

IV. **PRESENTING:** Call on someone from each group to read the group's draft.
   A. Comment on the good details and variety of approaches.
   B. Display the papers for further study and comparison.

LESSON SIX: WHAT IS GOOD WRITING?

Objectives: The students will be able to

- Examine student writing and recognize some elements of good writing (e.g., honesty, clarity).
- Practice choosing specific words.

Procedure:

I. Remind students one concern of this class is to define "good writing."
   A. Ask them to brainstorm about possible definitions. All points are recorded on the blackboard.
   B. Some suggestions are likely to be
      1. Interesting
      2. Has something to write about
      3. Says it clearly

II. Distribute a copy of the accompanying writing samples to each student. (Decide whether you wish students to keep and save all handouts.)
   A. Ask students to read each and decide which is the better writing and why?
   B. Most students will choose Writing 2. They are likely to answer:
      1. "Number 1 is so vague and too short."
      2. "Number 2 is funny; it made me smile; I used to do funny things like that."
      3. "Number 2 is a good story."

III. Encourage students to see that Writing 2 is a good story that becomes *good writing* because of the following:
   A. It is **honest:**
      - The author is not afraid to tell about something silly.
      - The author doesn't pretend to reach for big ideas.
      - The author writes about what she knows.
   B. It uses **specifics:**
      - For example, author states "we were four"; "my cousin Scott"; "a big spider, five worms, and a potato bug."
      - Author uses direct dialogue.
   C. It **has a focus:**
      - Instead of many generalized incidents, she writes about *one time* and *makes the reader see it.*

IV. Introduce a practice exercise for using facts and specific words and phrases to show rather than tell.
   A. Some words are general and stand for groups. "Furniture" is general and "bunk bed" is specific.
   B. Write a general word on the chalkboard, such as "liquid."
   C. Ask students to brainstorm for specific words such as "battery

acid" or "instant coffee." Expect each student to furnish an example.

    D. Next, begin with the word "car." Call on a student on one side of the room to begin a description with good facts. Move on to the next student and the next until every class member has contributed to the description. This is fun and students love it. Urge them to be specific: "What's on the windshield?" "Show us more about the fender." They will produce humorous, specific descriptions.

If time allows: Repeat the last exercise using a second word such as "road."

Name _____ Date _____

1.4 Writing Samples

WRITING 1

It's not easy to be a teenager. There are a lot more problems and worries as you get older. For example, I have many more responsibilities, and the school work is tougher, too. I often look back on my childhood and wish I were young and carefree again. My cousin and I used to have happy times together. We were always investigating things and getting into trouble. Whenever I see him now, we remember the things we used to do and laugh a lot.

Chad

WRITING 2

When my cousin, Scott, and I were little, we were always investigating things and getting into trouble. Once, when we were four, we were playing in the sand box. I found a big spider, five worms, and a potato bug. Scott made a house to keep them in while I showed my Aunt Giner our family of bugs. I couldn't figure out why she got so mad about a few bugs. She wouldn't even come over to me to look at them, so I went to see what Scott was up to. He had finished the house with some cardboard and sticks, and we sat down and talked for a while.

I told him, "I wish I had some makeup just like my mom's."

He replied, "I wish I could do something that no one else would do, so I could be called 'brave'." Then Scott told me that they must make makeup out of worms, because when he broke one apart, red stuff came out. Well, that's when it hit me. I could use worms for makeup! I broke one apart and smeared it on my cheeks and lips. It worked well, but my lipstick tasted sour.

Scott said, "You look pretty! Now, think of something I can do to be brave."

I sat thinking for a few minutes and then I said, "I haven't heard of anybody eating a spider before. That would be brave, because I bet it really tastes icky."

Scott thought about it for a while and finally he said, "O.K."

I had to play Mommy again. I went and got a plate, fork, and napkin. Then I pretended to cook food. When it was all ready I called, "Supper's ready."

Scott came over and just looked for a long time. Then he picked up the mashed spider with a fork, put it in his mouth and swallowed it. He didn't even smile. He just said, "You overcooked it. It tastes yucky."

We were like that when we were little. Now we just look back and laugh a lot.

Dawn

LESSON SEVEN: SHOWING, NOT TELLING

Objectives: The students will be able to

- Review choice of specific words.
- Use listing as a prewriting activity.
- Practice writing with facts and specific details in Freewriting 4.

Procedure:

I. Review the concept of showing rather than telling.
- A. Write the sentence, "It was a pretty crummy place," on the blackboard.
- B. Ask the class to decide what the place is to be (a building or particular locale, for example).
- C. Go around the room asking each student to supply a specific detail to add to the description.
- D. Record each person's answer on the board.
- E. A sample brainstorming might look like this:

House

broken chimney, fallen bricks, gray weathered wood, all windows broken, one covered with cardboard, grayed curtains blowing at the windows, knee-high grass, broken cement sidewalk, wooden steps falling away from front door, garbage and paper litter cought in wire fence, water pump in yard, tin cup at its base, "condemned" written on sign on front door.

II. **DRAFTING:** Explain *Freewriting 4*.
- A. Make a copy of the following telling sentences:
  1. My teacher is strict.
  2. There were many interesting costumes at the party.
  3. It looked like a haunted house.
  4. The puppy is undisciplined.
  5. Spring will soon be here.
  6. My mother bugs me.
  7. This school has great school spirit.
  8. This school has terrible school spirit.
  9. School lunches are unbelievably bad.
  10. He was shy.
  11. It was a great game.
  12. My sister doesn't trust me.
  13. The children were having fun.
  14. School is so boring.
  15. It's not easy to be a freshman (or sophomore, or junior, or senior).

16. The principal is unfair.
17. My father was really mad.
18. It was a wonderful date.
19. She is such a snob.
20. She's the school's best athlete.
21. This has been a bad winter.
22. The old man is lonely.
23. The substitute teacher was strange.
24. My little brother is nosy.
25. He was embarrassed.
26. She was exhausted.
27. It was a friendly dog.
28. I loved that class.
29. She seems to be worried.
30. Owning a car is a nuisance.

B. Cut out the sentences so each is on a single piece of paper.
C. Place the sentences in a container, and pass it around the room, asking each student to draw out one sentence.
D. Explain that each sentence is a telling sentence. The students' assignment is to turn the telling sentences into effective showing paragraphs.
E. Encourage each student to brainstorm a list of details before beginning a draft.
F. Students should understand they are to use all of the remainder of the period for listing, brainstorming, and drafting independently. **Insist there be no talking during a writing time. Make this a consistent rule.**
G. You may wish to require that students not use the original words of the telling sentence in their showing writing.

Adapted from *Writers in Training* by Rebekah Caplan (Palo Alto, CA: Dale Seymour Publication 1984), used by permission.

LESSON EIGHT: REVISING AND SHARING

Objective: The students will be able to

- Revise and share a draft of a paragraph.

Procedure:

  I. Review the concept of telling and showing.
 II. **REVISING:** Ask the students to examine their Freewriting 4. Encourage them to add additional specific words or facts and to revise their paragraphs in any way necessary to read them aloud to their classmates.
III. **PRESENTING:**
  A. Have the students take turns reading their drafts aloud.
  B. Call upon those who are listening to a reading to recall details, words, or phrases which are particularly vivid and which they "see" best.
  C. When everyone has read, remind students to place Freewriting 4 in their folders.

If there is additional time:

- Write another telling sentence on the board: "The bus ride was uncomfortable."
- Ask students to turn this sentence into a showing paragraph.
- Students may be asked to volunteer to read these paragraphs at the beginning of the next class period.

LESSON NINE: EXPANDING A STORY

Objectives: The students will be able to

- Review terminology and definitions.
- Practice sentence expansion.
- Invent and expand a story in Freewriting 5.

Procedure:

I. Review the concept of showing rather than telling. If students wrote a second paragraph in Lesson Eight, call for volunteers to read their showing paragraphs based on *The bus ride was uncomfortable.*

II. **PREWRITING:** Introduce the following prewriting exercise.

    A. Write the sentence, *He got up,* at the top of the blackboard.

    B. Write the sentence, *He went downstairs,* as far beneath the first sentence as possible.

    C. Ask the students in a whole class activity to expand the writing by inserting facts and specific details. The sentence may become

Jim struggled out of bed, tossing back the gray, frayed sheets and placed his feet, one at a time, on the bare, wooden floor. His head throbbed as he reached for the alarm clock tipped on its side beneath the bed. It was noon and hot. Outside the window, the pine trees along the lakeshore seemed to float in a sparkling mirage, and a motor boat roared in the distance. . . .

III. **DRAFTING** *Freewriting 5:*

    A. A sample direction:

> Place the sentence, "He started up the sidewalk" on the top line of your paper. On the bottom of the page write, "Finally, he knocked on the door." For fifteen minutes, fill in the space between the sentences by expanding the story with facts and specific details. When the freewriting is done and if there is time, reread and make any necessary changes.

    B. Write with the students.

IV. **REVISING:** Give students time to edit briefly.

V. **SHARING:** When all students have finished writing, ask for volunteers to read aloud their drafts, or call on as many people as possible. Everyone enjoys hearing a variety of these papers. Another sentence option for this exercise is "The phone rang./She answered it."

LESSON TEN: LISTING, REHEARSING, AND DRAFTING

Objectives: The students will be able to

- Practice listing as a brainstorming activity.
- Rehearse their ideas with another student.
- Use a specific, personal experience in Freewriting 6.

Procedure:

I. **PREWRITING:** Introduce the following activity.
   A. Ask the students to write the heading "childhood memories" at the top of their papers.
   B. Have them list words or phrases referring to memories from their past which are possible writing topics.
   C. Encourage the students to make their lists as long as possible.
   D. Read a sample writing based on a childhood memory. (Eric's final draft in Part One, Chapter Four, is one option.)
   E. After the sample is read, have students list additional ideas which come to mind.
   F. Finally, ask students to choose one memory from their lists, and zero in on it, again listing as many details surrounding that memory as possible.

II. **REHEARSING**
   A. Pair off students and ask each to explain (rehearse) the memory out loud to a partner. This helps writers to focus their ideas and purpose.
   B. Encourage partners to ask appropriate questions for clarification.
   C. You may wish to model this technique with a student before asking the entire class to do it.

III. **DRAFTING** *Freewriting 6:*

Write freely for fifteen to twenty minutes or longer, if necessary, about a specific experience or childhood memory. Write about one time, using facts and specific details. Include items from your brainstorming list, but also allow yourself to remember and discover new facts and details which you will "see" again as you write. When you have sustained the writing as long as possible, reread. Make any necessary changes or adjustments. Use the checklist on the blackboard to aid you as you revise. Do not interrupt or talk with other students, but use all the remaining time to work independently and quietly.

IV. **REVISING:** Checklist for the blackboard.
   A. Did I write about one time?
   B. Did I use facts and specific details?
   C. Will an audience understand and see?

V. At the end of the period, students return their papers to the folders. Explain that this writing is still in the drafting stage and additional time will be available for further revision.

Some additional suggestions:

1. *Students should understand they have the option to write about topics other than what is being suggested.* They are, however, always expected to attempt the skills mentioned.

2. Be aware that writing exercises can penalize the most thoughtful student, the one who sees countless possibilities open to him. Fluency is always one goal, of course, but some writers need lots of time.

3. Some students may need your help getting started. For example, two students have blank papers after five minutes. One student may simply have a careful, more leisurely composing style. The second may be stuck, and this is the student who needs your help. You may remind the second student that it's all right not to come up with something on a particular day, or you may ask questions to elicit his or her words or ideas which are then written down. As a last resort, supply starter words or a beginning sentence.

LESSON ELEVEN: AUDIENCE

Objectives: The students will be able to

- Become better acquainted through an interview and writing exercise.
- Differentiate between personal writing and traditional school writing.
- Begin to understand how writing is adjusted for particular audiences.

Procedure:

I. **PREWRITING:** Introduce the following get acquainted, writing exercise.

    A. Number half the students. Begin numbering a second time. Ask those students with the same number to move together to work in pairs. (If numbers are uneven, you should become a part of this exercise, also.)

    B. Ask the pairs to take turns interviewing one another. Remind them to take notes.

    C. Each interviewer will be given six minutes to ask questions. After the time has elapsed, the roles will be reversed and the second student will be given another six minutes to interview his or her partner.

II. **DRAFTING:**

    A. After the interviewing is completed, ask students to write a recipe for each partner.

    B. Discuss the format of a recipe and brainstorm for examples of terminology.

    C. Place the following sample on the blackboard:

To create Melissa

Combine:

    1 head of curly brown hair
    1 set of sparkling green eyes
    2 dangling silver earrings
    1 best friend named Kris
    a love of reading
    a dash of smiles

Mix thoroughly and sprinkle with a
dream of becoming a psychologist. Simmer for 17 years and serve.

III. **PRESENTING:** After students have had sufficient time for drafting and revision (but during the same class period, if possible) have all the students read the recipes for their partners aloud. This is fun but less so, if the reading is carried over to a second day. If you wish, each recipe may be given to the person about whom it is written.

IV. **An activity to emphasize the concept of audience:**
  A. Ask the students to write a personal note to their partners on the topic: "What I think about this class right now." Assure them that the partner is the only person who will ever see the note. When the notes are completed, they are delivered to the intended audience.
  B. Have the students write again on the same topic. This time the audience will be the teacher. Students are to write brief paragraphs as if they expect them to be graded.
  C. Collect the teacher papers and read anonymous samples aloud.
  D. Discuss: How does the intended audience affect a writing?
  1. The note: Although only two students have seen each note, the notes are probably:
    a. Written in informal language.
    b. Concerned with ideas; however, the writers may have written about another topic entirely.
    c. Less concerned with form, mechanical correctness, or neatness.
  2. The teacher paper
    a. Is written to please the teacher.
    b. Has more formal language.
    c. Has more emphasis placed on form, mechanical correctness, and neatness.
  3. Conclusion: Effective writers know their audiences and write with the audience in mind.

LESSON TWELVE: INFLATED LANGUAGE

Objectives: The students will be able to

- Understand that good writers write clearly and honestly.
- Recognize euphemisms, jargon, and cliches and work to substitute new, fresh words and phrases.

Procedure:

I. Write the words, "euphemism," "jargon," and "cliche" on the blackboard.

II. Ask students to define the words, if possible.

III. Point out that good writers write honestly, avoiding misleading phrases, inflated language, and worn-out expressions.

IV. Hand out the worksheets that follow, **Euphemisms, Jargon,** and **Cliches,** and spend time going through them. Ask the students to complete each exercise.

Answers for worksheet questions:

<u>Euphemisms</u> ("inoperable statements" are *lies,* "cross-border incursion training exercises" are *invasions*):

(1) A life jacket—*flotation device;* (2) A garbage dump—*a sanitary landfill;* (3) Sweat—*perspiration;* (4) A politician—*a statesman;* (5) The Department of War—*the Department of Defense.* Three more: mechanics may be called *maintenance personnel,* the Korean conflict was called a *police action,* and the war in Viet nam has been called a *peace-keeping mission.*

<u>Jargon:</u>

This object is a pencil.

It's a shovel.

It's a snowball.

<u>Cliches:</u>

Options to replace cliches: (1) a shadow fall, your heart beat, or an ant sneeze; (2) reads books backward; (3) a box of kittens; (4) a cockroach; (5) the ketchup that lost the race; (6) a sunset; (7) the ants in the attic/or the dust bunnies bounce; (8) superman; (9) bleached bedsheets; (10) nails.

1.5 Euphemisms

People write to communicate. Good writers express themselves clearly in fresh, new ways. They write honestly, avoiding misleading phrases, inflated language, and worn-out expressions.

Euphemisms (from the Greek "to speak fair") are mild or indirect words or expressions substituted for those thought to be too harsh or offensive. The phrase "passed away" is substituted for "died," or "funeral director" may be substituted for "undertaker." Sometimes euphemisms are used to make something sound more important. "Janitor" becomes "custodian" and "garbage collector" becomes "sanitation worker." In advertising, nothing is "cheap"; it's "affordable."

In many cases euphemisms are harmless, but they can also be deliberately misleading. When the spaceship *Challenger* exploded, a NASA announcer explained there had been "a major malfunction." Government and military officials have often been criticized for using euphemisms to hide the truth. Propaganda becomes "disinformation activities," and murder becomes "termination with extreme prejudice." Critics say that such language prevents people from finding out what they need to know. Would you know what is meant by "inoperable statements" or "cross-border incursion training exercises"?

Can you complete the following euphemisms?

1. A life jacket is a _____

2. A garbage dump is a _____

3. Sweat is _____

4. A politician is a _____

5. The Department of War is now the Department of _____

Can you think of three more?

1. _____

2. _____

3. _____

Name _____ Date _____

1.6 Jargon

Jargon is "insider" language that people in trades or professions use. Sometimes writers use this language for general audiences, thinking it sounds impressive and important. In reality, it often prevents writers from communicating clearly. Computer and space program jargon has become popular. Sometimes we hear that rather than talking with one another, two people "interface" with one another.

Below are three descriptions of ordinary objects written in the jargon of the space program. Can you identify the objects?

1. This object is a data-imprint system, known as DIS. It's a graphite linear feed designed to perform a message-recording function. It is protected by a cellulose-fiber reinforced-resin layer, and in the expunge mode, the opposite end of the machine is briskly rubbed across the characters to be eliminated.

This object is a _____

2. This object is a portable, unitized earthwork system also called a terrestrial transport shuttle. When low-level personnel assume a command control function, earth is relocated with the air to ground adjustment probe.

It's a _____

3. This Spherical Deterrent-Device (SDD) is manually constructed on site from one part oxygen and two parts hydrogen in a solid state. Its operational mode is activated by a coordinated contraction and expansion of the biceps and triceps muscles. Its inherent self-destructing capability is activated at 0° centigrade and increases proportionately to a relative increment in temperature. It is rarely, if ever, found in tropic or sub-tropic climes, but if you do find it there, be sure to duck.

It's a _____

1.7 Cliches

Cliches were once fresh new expressions that were so popular they became worn out or trite. Notice how many of the following you will be able to identify immediately.

blind as a _____ mind like a _____ cry like a _____

flat as a _____ eats like a _____ went over like a _____

on pins and _____ they're dropping like _____ light as a _____

sticks out like a _____ the news spread like _____

The trouble with cliches is that they become tired and predictable. They lose their force. A good writer avoids them and creates new ways, startling ways, to describe objects and people. Complete the following sentences with the strongest, most original comparisons possible.

1. So quiet you could hear _____

2. My little brother is so nosy he _____

3. As busy as a _____

4. He's quicker than a _____

5. They're as slow as _____

6. Her face turned as red as _____

7. The guests grew so quiet you could hear _____

8. He was faster than _____

9. She was as white as _____

10. He had a heart of _____

LESSON THIRTEEN: SELF-EVALUATION AND REVISION

Objective: The students will be able to

- Evaluate and revise a freewriting (Revision 1) for an audience of their peers.

Procedure:

This activity may take *several class periods*. Give students plenty of time to complete their revisions.

I. Review the term "audience" as it relates to writing.

II. Explain to students they are to choose one of their freewritings (1–6).

III. Explain they will be given time and help in their revisions, and when the revisions are completed, they will read their writings to the whole class in the large circle.

IV. Remind students that "revision" means "to see again," to change the writing in any way necessary to present to a particular audience.

V. Give each student the accompanying **Self-Evaluation Checklist for Revision 1**. (Other elements will be included in subsequent checklists.)

VI. Confer individually with students. (See Part One, Chapter Four, Student-Teacher Conferences.) It is easy to overedit. Work to maintain each writer's style.

    A. It is important during the early drafts to deemphasize mechanical correctness. As a writing nears completion, however, you may suggest some final copy requirements such as

        1. Write in ink on one side of unlined paper.

        2. Give your paper a title.

        3. Observe adequate margins.

        4. Check the paragraphing.

        5. Edit for spelling and punctuation.

        6. Sign your name at the end of your writing (as an author would do).

    B. If a grade is to be given, evaluate only the final draft. A grade should reflect the student's ability to use specific facts and details. How well does the writer show rather than tell?

Name _____   Date _____

1.8 Self-evaluation Checklist For Revision 1

The third stage of the writing process is revision and editing. It is the time when a writer changes and polishes the freewriting in any way necessary to present it to a particular audience. This stage is not always easy, because it is difficult to step back and look at our writing objectively. As this class continues, you will become more skilled as an editor. However, in the beginning it is helpful to pretend you have never seen your writing before. Look at the draft with "new eyes," keeping the passages which are good and omitting those which are unnecessary and repetitious. Don't try to fix everything at once. A better strategy for revision is to choose one or two elements to work on and stay with them through the whole piece.

The following is a list of questions for you to consider as you revise and edit your paper:

1. The purpose of my paper is _____

2. Have I reread this paper as if I have never seen it before? _____

3. Does it make sense? _____ Will the audience understand? _____

4. Did I write about one time? _____

5. Did I use facts and specific words and phrases? _____ Can I add more? ____

6. Will the audience "see"? _____

7. Have I kept the good passages? _____ The best part of my paper is _____

   _____

8. Have I written honestly? Have I avoided euphemisms, jargon, and cliches? _

   _____

   _____

   _____

   _____

LESSON FOURTEEN: LISTENING

Objective: The students will be able to

• Recognize the duties and characteristics of good listeners

Procedure

I. Introduce a class warm-up exercise.
   A. Round-the-room game: Have each student *try* to say "unique New York" three times (fun!).
   B. Animal Dominoes—one student names an animal. The next student names a second animal whose name begins with the last letter of the previously mentioned animal. The activity continues around the room.

II. Explain to the class that this day's activities are concerned with listening and the characteristics of good listeners. The exercise is in preparation for upcoming work in large and small circles where students will be expected to be good listeners.

III. Arrange the class in groups of two. Suggest students find a partner in the group whom they do not know well, or number the students off.
   A. Place suggested topics for discussion on the blackboard:
      1. The dream vacation I'd like to take.
      2. What it's like to grow up in a small town, a large city, an ethnic neighborhood (choose one).
      3. The proudest moment of my life and why.
      4. What I'd like to accomplish in my life and why.
      5. What I remember most about my parents.
      6. Your own subject, if nothing here appeals to you.
   B. Direct one student in each pair to speak with his or her partner on a chosen topic or topics for five minutes. The second student is to listen and *encourage* the speaker.
   C. After the time has elapsed, have the students exchange roles for another five minutes.
   D. For a brief time (45 seconds–1 minute), have students again exchange roles. Tell the student acting as a listener to give *negative* feedback.
   E. Repeat.

IV. Have students return to their desks. In a round-the-room session, ask the following questions:
   What did your partner do to encourage you as a speaker?
   What did your partner do to discourage you as a speaker?
   Tell us one *new* bit of information you learned about your partner?

81

V. The class may arrive at definitions similar to the following:
   A. Good listeners
      1. are supportive and kind.
      2. let the speaker know they hear what is being said.
      3. ask useful, interesting questions.
      4. show they are interested.
      5. look at the speaker.
   B. Poor listeners
      1. interrupt.
      2. criticize or argue.
      3. concentrate on another activity.
      4. speak to someone else.

LESSON FIFTEEN: PEER RESPONSE

Objectives: The students will be able to

- Act as an audience for their peers.
- Respond to the writing of their peers

Procedure:

This activity will take at least *two class periods.*

    I. Hand out the accompanying **Directions for Students in the Large Group.** Explain the sheet and answer any questions.

    II. Have the students arrange their desks in a large circle.

    III. Ask two or three large circle questions as a warm-up exercise. (see Part One, Chapter Four, The Large Circle.) On this day, ask one student to begin a story. Explain that each student in the circle is to add a sentence with new information. The goal is to sustain the story around the entire circle. This is fun and may be used more than once for a class warm-up. With practice, students become more skillful.

    IV. Students may volunteer or take turns reading Revision 1.

    V. After each reading, peers are asked to respond. If no one volunteers, call on other students in the circle, "John, what do you like about Jim's writing?" or "What did you *see* best?" Students are initially shy to make comments but are more and more willing to do so as they gain confidence. The goal is to help students learn to make legitimate responses to the writing of others, and this is a skill they can learn in time.

A suggestion: For this first reading in the large circle, students are to keep their revision checklist in mind but are asked to point out only **the good elements** of each writing. To keep the first sharing experience positive, all remarks about weaknesses should be reserved for later revisions. Encourage students to respond both honestly and specifically. Discourage statements such as, "I liked the description." Instead, insist they cite specific words or phrases.

    Note: The students will be expected to complete self-evaluations of their revisions in Lessons Thirty-three and Forty-three. They will also choose one revision to polish further in Lesson Forty-four, and all revisions will be published in a personal booklet at the end of Unit Six or Unit Ten. With this in mind, you may wish to collect all final drafts to ensure that copies are not lost. Also: Remind students they will need a single-subject notebook for their journals in Lesson Sixteen.

Name _____ Date _____

1.9 Directions For Students in the Large Group

1. When directed to do so by the teacher, move your desk as quietly as possible into a large circle. You should be able to see the face of every other student.

2. The teacher begins by asking one or two circle questions.

3. You are encouraged to volunteer to read your paper. If no one volunteers, the teacher will call on students to read.

4. You are *expected* to have your revisions completed and ready to read at the beginning of a day designated for the large circle. No one should be working on or copying a paper while another student is reading.

5. If for some reason you come into class late and another student is reading, wait quietly by the door until the reading is completed. Then *quietly* pull a desk into the circle. Do not talk to others as you do so.

6. Remember, the purpose of the large and small circles is to

> Be supportive and kind.
> Let the writer know that you hear
> Tell the writer what you like (be specific).
> Ask questions.
> Help the writer to improve

It is *not* a time to

> Attack or criticize.
> Interrupt.
> Concentrate on another activity
> Speak to someone else.

7 At the end of the class period or when directed to do so, return your desk to its original place and hand in your final draft to the teacher.

unit 2

FURTHER WORK WITH
THE WRITING PROCESS

Lessons Sixteen through Twenty-six in this unit introduce journal writing, clustering as a prewriting activity, and editing for economy and punctuation. Students do two freewritings and choose one to edit further as Revision 2. The lessons take the student writers through the entire writing process and conclude with the publication of a class booklet.

LESSON SIXTEEN: JOURNAL WRITING

Objectives: The students will be able to
- Understand the advantages of journal writing.
- Write a journal entry of their own.

Procedure:

I. Introduce the journal.
  A. People have been keeping journals and diaries for centuries.
    1. Thoreau, *Walden.*
    2. Anne Frank, *Diary of a Young Girl.*
    3. John Steinbeck, *Travels with Charley.*
  B. Journals have been important to writers.
    1. E. B. White: "Usually, when a man quits writing in his journal . . . he has lost interest in life."
    2. Ralph Waldo Emerson: "Keep a journal. Pay so much honor to the visits of truth to your mind as to record them."
    3. Henry David Thoreau: "The journal is a record of experience and growth, not a preserve of things well done or said."
II. Explain your expectations for student journals. (See Part One, Chapter Three.)
  A. Journals provide scheduled practice in freewriting.
    1. Some entries will be excellent.
    2. Other attempts will be weak.
  B. Journals offer a risk-free setting.
    1. They are never corrected or graded.
    2. They are read by the teacher who may comment in writing.
  C. Journals are not a place for secrets (as a diary may be).
    1. When in the possession of the teacher, journals are read by no one else.
    2. Writers may share their entries with others but are never forced to do so.
    3. Writers may fold the page over or write "don't read" alongside entries they do not wish the teacher to read.
  D. Journals are honest and truthful.
  E. Journals are a place to experiment with language and explore ideas.
  F. Journals help writers to discover writing topics for class assignments.
  G. Journals are a place to make observations.
  H. Journals are a collection of writing done over a period of time.
    1. Writers see progress.

      2. Writers see ideas develop and change.

      3. Writers see themselves with greater perspective and understanding.

  I. The writing workshop journal:

      1. Students write in a standard-size, one-subject notebook.

      2. Entries are numbered consecutively (may also be dated).

      3. Most entries are five to six minute freewritings covering about two-thirds of a notebook page.

      4. Journals are collected every two weeks (usually on Friday and returned the following Monday).

      5. Students are encouraged to make a habit of carrying their journals with them.

      6. In the workshop, journal writing is primarily an out-of-class activity.

III. Read the following sample journal entries by students; emphasize that strong entries such as these do not occur every time a journalist writes.

JOURNAL 48

In first grade my friend Joe had a pair of salamanders. He brought them in for Show and Tell and then just left them at school. Everyone fought over who got to feed them. Soon it was Christmas vacation. We came back to find two crisp, dry salamanders. Joe was all upset. He put water on them and thought they would be o.k. They weren't. They were stiff like little dead leaves and ones' leg broke off. It wasn't funny then.

                                                  John

JOURNAL 24

"Something just ran across the road," Mom said.

"What is it?" my sister asked.

We pulled over and backed up. Dad and I got out of the car and started to walk back. Dad knew what it was. We searched the area, and then we saw it. It was a baby killdeer. It was light brown with black streaks on it. It ran like a giraffe. Not because its neck is long but because its legs are full size when it's born. I walked as fast as I could after the baby, watching not to step on it. It squawked to its mother, and she ran over. She screeched and flopped on her side. With one wing in the air, she spun around on the ground. We watched the mother and then went back to find the baby. It had fallen down, and I carefully picked it up. It was like a fluffy, cotton ball. A little peep shook its body. The mother squawked and led the rest of her babies across the road.

"Let's go," Dad said.

I carefully set the baby down, and it peeped and cheeped its way
across the road to its mama. In a couple of seconds they were gone.

Lortie

IV. Give students time to write their first five- to six-minute journal entry.
You may make a suggestion for a topic. For example,
   A. Place the words "simple pleasure" on the blackboard.
   B. Give an example of a simple pleasure in your own life.
   C. Ask students to freewrite a journal entry about something that is a
      simple pleasure in their lives (or pick a topic of their own). They
      should always understand they have the option of picking their own
      topics.

V. Hand out and discuss the accompanying list of suggestions, Topics for
Beginning a Journal.

VI. Encourage students to add their own ideas to this list of possible journal
topics.

2.1 Topics for Beginning a Journal

What goes into a journal? Anything you wish to include. Entries may be observations, memories, dreams, questions, new words, letters, anecdotes, lists, poems, stories, descriptions, conversations, ideas, the trivial, or the silly.

The journal can be whatever the writer wishes it to be. Most of all it is a place to try, practice, experiment, and find writing topics. A person who keeps a journal joins an ancient literary tradition—and creates a fresh one.

SUGGESTIONS:

1. Describe yourself as your best friend would describe you.
2. What are three of the nicest things others have said about you?
3. Describe a friend.
4. What are some things that make you unique?
5. If you could live in another time in history, what would you choose and why?
6. Write about a funny dream.
7. Describe a nightmare.
8. Write from the viewpoint of your pencil (your shoe, your pet, your desk). Describe the world from a new perspective.
9. Record overheard conversations in a classroom, the halls, a school bus.
10. Turn a telling sentence into a showing paragraph, for example, "A job is a learning experience."
11. Write about a disagreement between yourself and someone else. How do people know when you are angry?
12. Write about telling a lie you did not regret (or one you later regretted).
13. Write about your childhood secret places.
14. Write about a time a parent was worried but tried to hide it from you.
15. Assume that your journal will be read 250 years from now. Write an entry that communicates to future readers something interesting about you and the time in which you live.
16. Write a series of entries all beginning with "I remember . . . ."
17. Write a letter to yourself from a relative no longer living.
18. Do you have a cookie person (someone from your childhood who would give you cookies to eat even if it were almost mealtime)? Describe the person and your relationship.
19. The writer James Baldwin pointed out, "The one face that one can never see is one's own face." What do you suppose he meant by this? How do you *see* yourself?

20. The first time we do anything is always memorable. Describe one of your "first times" (riding a bike, swimming, babysitting, being alone).

21. Describe the *last* time you did something terrifying, or embarrassing.

22. Write about how to do something: wash dishes, wait in line, primp, make a phone call, clean your room, ask for money, ask for a date, save money, get caught, apologize, make a friend, be a *real* freshman (sophomore, junior, senior).

23. Write about scars, seen and unseen.

24. Write about childhood losses.

25. Describe a tour of your neighborhood (as a pet, a mail carrier, an alien).

LESSON SEVENTEEN: BRAINSTORMING

Objective: The students will be able to

• Use listing, rehearsing, and brainstorming as prewriting activities for Freewriting 7.

Procedure:

The following exercises are designed to help students find a topic, discover a quantity of ideas, and practice brainstorming.

  I. **PREWRITING:** Introduce Freewriting 7, a grade school memory.

      A. Students should understand this topic is simply one option, and they may choose any topic they wish.

      B. Read the following sample of a writing about a school memory.

Fourth Grade

Whenever I think of grade school, I am in Mrs. Molland's Fourth Grade Room in Reeder, North Dakota. My parents had returned to North Dakota from California the previous summer, and my mother worried about my starting school in the fall. California's schools were supposed to be progressive, and, at that time "progressive" meant lots of reading, art, and music.

After California, my school in North Dakota was a shock. There were only fifteen students in our room, but we made up grades three, four, and five. Because I was a fourth grader, I sat in the middle row of the room, which smelled of chalk, musty books, and dusty geraniums. On rainy or winter days, the cloak room, lined with coats and rubber boots, smelled of peanut butter and moth balls.

One day, early in the year, Mrs. Molland, a tall, bony, red-haired woman, began our arithmetic class. "Phyllis Olson," she said, "go to the board and do problem three. Mary, you do number four, and Richard, do number five.

We walked to the blackboard. Phyllis and Richard worked quickly. Their chalk clicked and squeaked as they worked. I just looked at my book and then at the board. "Add these numbers, Mary," Mrs. Molland said. I did that. "Fine," she said, "now divide by three."

I turned from the board and said, "I don't know what you mean."

Everyone in the room stopped his school work to look at me. "Mean?" Her voice got higher, "I mean divide by three."

"I don't know what 'divide' means."

"What's wrong with you," she said, "a fourth grader! Why even the third graders know what 'divide' means." She pointed to the third grade row. "Evelyn, do the problem for Mary." So Evelyn walked to the board and made some marks there. They seemed to please Mrs. Molland.

I remember staring straight at the board, salty tears dripping from my nose and chin, afraid to turn around and have the others see me cry. And I remember going home at lunch time and insisting, "I'm never going back."

However, return I did, and that same night and for many nights to come, my grandfather became my tutor. We added, subtracted, multiplied, *and* divided. I argued, "Dividing is dumb," but even so, he taught me to do it.

Mary

II. Ask students to list on paper incidents and memories they recall from their own grade school experiences that are possible writing topics.

III. Lead a brainstorming session which will help students add to their initial lists. Have the students write words and phrases in response to the following directions.

    A. Name some schools you've attended.
    B. Did you have a favorite? Least favorite? Why?
    C. Recall some of your teachers by name. Favorite? Least favorite? Why?
    D. Recall a time you felt happy about yourself in school.
    E. Recall a time you felt bad about yourself in school.
    F. Recall a time someone was picked on or mistreated.
    G. Recall a school punishment you deserved.
    H. Recall a school punishment you did not deserve.
    I. List some sounds you associate with school.
    J. List some smells you associate with school.
    K. Think of something a teacher said over and over.
    L. Think of some advice someone gave you about school.
    M. Describe a report card.
    N. What did you most enjoy in the school day?
    O. Who was one of your best friends in school. Why?
    P. How did you get to school?
    Q. Describe a favorite piece of clothing you wore to school.
    R. How did you spend recess?
    S. Think of the names of some of the students:
       1. Who was the "worst" student in school?
       2. Who was the "best" student in school?
       3. Did you have an "enemy"? Why?
       4. Was there a bully? Who?

IV. Ask the students to zero in on one incident.

    A. Decide on a general incident about which you will write.

       B. List all the facts you can remember.

       C. Exaggerate if you wish.

       D. Borrow incidents from another time.

V. **REHEARSING:** Have students explain the topic they have chosen to a partner. The partner may ask questions about anything which seems unclear. (Another option: After the partners have finished and before students begin their freewriting, have each student describe his plan to the entire class.)

VI. **DRAFTING** Freewriting 7: A sample direction.

Look over your brainstorming list, and when you are ready, begin your freewriting. Write about one time, using as many facts and specific details as possible. Allow yourself the chance to discover new details and facts as you write. You will have the remainder of the class period for writing. If you finish early, reread your writing and make changes and additions, but do not speak with or interrupt other students.

VII. At the end of the period, have students place their freewriting in their folders and return these folders to the designated spot. Students should understand they are to do this whenever they complete a freewriting.

LESSON EIGHTEEN: CLUSTERING

Objectives: The students will be able to

- Learn to cluster as a prewriting activity.
- Cluster in preparation for a freewriting.
- Complete Freewriting 8 based on a cluster.

Procedure:

I. **PREWRITING:** Introduce students to the concept of clustering. (See Part One, Chapter Three.)
  A. Explain clustering (a tool similar to brainstorming which enables writers to discover new ideas).
  B. Model and demonstrate a cluster on the blackboard. Use a word such as *dream* as the stimulus word.

II. Next, ask the class to practice a cluster as a whole class activity.
  A. Encircle a word such as *afraid* on the blackboard and ask, "What do you think of when you see this word?"
  B. Write down all the student responses (cluster) radiating outward.
  C. When the students have finished giving their responses, point out the many ideas the class has discovered.

III. Have the students choose a stimulus word of their own and cluster independently for as long as possible. Encourage them to continue the cluster until they discover an idea they feel they need to write about. (Some possible stimulus words for students who need help are *grandpa, still, dark, goodbye, family, time, loss, help.*)

IV. **DRAFTING:** *Freewriting 8*

When the cluster is completed, have students use the remainder of the period to write. The students should understand that they have a large amount of material and that not everything will be included in the freewriting. The freewriting, itself, may take them in new directions.

V. Encourage students to try additional clusters *after* completing a free-writing. This will aid them in further focusing a writing.

LESSON NINETEEN: PRACTICING PEER RESPONSE

Objectives: The students will be able to

- Pick out good elements in student writing.
- Make specific suggestions for improving student writing.

Procedure:

I. RESPONDING

    A. Distribute copies of **Student Writing Samples,** or make transparencies and display the writings on the overhead projector. Explain that these samples are early drafts of students' writings.

    B. Ask the students to discuss the strengths and weaknesses of each. What advice can they give each student to help make each writing better?

    C. Use the following format:

        1. What do you like about the writing? (What do you see best?)

        2. What questions do you have about the writing?

        3. What suggestions do you have for making the writing better?

    D. Talk about useful comments which help a writer.

    E. Focus on the positive.

    F. Explain that the students will be expected to respond to one another's writings in this manner in the small circle (Lesson Twenty-one).

A comment: An entirely new type of learning situation is created as students are asked to evaluate the writing of others, a role they may never have had before. Don't expect too much at once. Students need practice, but in time they will become better editors of their own and the writing of others. Zero in on one skill at a time.

Some possible responses to the student papers:

Sample 1:

    1. The scene in which you get the runner out at third is good. You may want to expand it even more.

    2. No questions.

    3. Work on the beginning and ending. The first paragraph gives your story away. Do you need the first paragraph?

Sample 2:

    1. You have so many good facts and details such as exact names (Lincoln School, Jessica, Mrs. Lyle) and brand names such as Superfriends lunchboxes. The exact words of speakers is also good.

2. Did you ever eat the peanut butter bread? The ending is unclear.

3. Organize your story. When you mention the janitor the first time, it seemed as if you were already going outside. Get rid of any details that don't add to the story.

Sample 3:

1. It's funny. You make us laugh. I like the phrase "known nose picker." Your details like "Tonka trucks" and "blurred figures" are good.

2. Didn't you care how Randy felt, or doesn't that matter in this story?

3. Begin editing for spelling and punctuation.

2.2 Student Writing Samples

1. A Great Experience

Moving to Arizona for one year was a great experience. Well as far as baseball goes it was. I played for a team that the year before didn't win but one game. The season I got to play was great. We were picked to have a losing season for a second strait year. We finished winning twelve of fifteen games that season including the division championship.

That was a different story. To win the division we had to play what seemed like the hardest game of the season. We started by scoring seven runs in the first three innings, with our opponents scoring zero. In the last inning our opponents brought the score back to seven-six. They had runners on first and second with two outs.

With a hitter coming to the plate our coach calls time out. Walking to the mound he calls the infield in for a meeting. He told us that they will probably try and steel third. I was playing shortstop and a first year kid was playing third. The coach said if he steals Jesse was to backup and let me come over for the throw. And on the first pitch the runner took off for third, the throw from the catcher was right on the money. We nailed him to win seven-six. Everybody on the team went crazy. The celebration was probably the most exciting that that has ever happened to me.

Tom

2.2 Student Writing Samples (cont'd)

2. Peanut Butter

Before lunch time at Lincoln. Mrs. Johnson's first grade class would line up in the green carpeted hall. Boys in one line and girls in the other. Jessica, with her long red hair always stood next to me. As a class we would march down to the lunch room. Some would be carrying their Little House on the Prairie or Super-friends lunchboxes. As we entered the lunch room, we could hear Mrs. Lyle's class from 1A, already eating.

I led the girls line, past the cardboard pictures of apples, pears, hamburgers, that covered our cafeteria's walls. Nothing that they ever served here would look as good. The first cook placed a piece of burnt sausage pizza on my florescent orange tray. Next, they placed a huge serving of green mini-balls, otherwise known as peas. Then they place it, a slice of dry bread with peanut butter on it. I hated peanut butter with a passion. The smell was nauseating to me. And today all they had was 2% milk, no chocolate.

I picked up my silverware and walked past Mr. Kapp, a tall foreboding man, who was our janitor and watch dog during lunch. I hated this man who was inspecting our trays as we hurried outside for recess. I walked to a nearby table, sat and waited for Jess to sit beside me. Her pizza was the same as mine, black on top and flimsy on the bottom. Mrs. Carter was our monitor. She resembled a wolf circling it's prey.

Jess and I wolfed down our pizza, drank our milk and stuffed our peas in the milk containers, as usual. She ate her bread, and we marched up to the grey plastic garbage cans. Jess dumped her tray and headed out the door. I stepped to the can and heard, "Go back to the table and eat your bread.":

"I hate peanut butter," I answered.

"Sit down," he barked. I walked past the other tables and back past the children. As they laughed at me, the red hot tears of embarrasment began to flow down my face. I reached an empty table and sat down. I let the tears blur the scene around me. I could feel everyone staring at me. I just sat there feeling nauseated, tired and alone.

Finally, Mrs. Carter came over and picked up my tray and told me in a voice as cold as a crisp October morn, "Making a spectacle out of yourself, are ya? Well, you can just go sit in that green desk with your face turned towards the wall."

"I still won't eat it," I answered.

"Would you rather go to the principal's office?"

"No," I answered in a whisper. As a first grader, the word principal was like receiving the death sentence. I followed the witch, silently calling her names I'd heard my father use in times of extreme anger. I sat there, in that corner, closing my eyes and trying to picture myself outside playing 4 square with my friends.

I sat there for over an hour as the rest of Lincoln's classes had lunch and then recess. I started at the olive-drab desk, observed every detail, and went on to the next. I was allowed to go back to my class, walking slowly to the green plastic garbage can and finally dumped my tray.

Debbie

2.2 (cont'd)

3. Randy Germs

I walked into my kindergarten class, and saw all the kinds playing with the britely colored Tonka trucks, and running around playing tag a scream here and there when the girls get caught. I smiled, for today I was happy, because we were going on a field trip to the fire station. I get to see the big red shiny trucks, maybe I'll get to sit in one, I thought to myself. It's going to be so much fun. I put my long, plade coat, which I was so proud of, down on the floor, and ran to play with the other kids.

Soon I heard Mrs. Washington say "Pay attention." Everyone stopped what they were doing and ran to the front of the room where she was standing. We all had big, wide, eyes, filled with excitement. She said "Today is the day we go on our field trip, and I want everyone to pick a partner." Everyone immediately, ran off to pick a partner, before I even had a chance get up. I looked around sadly hoping that there would be some one left. There was no one, except for him, the nerd, the ever so disguisting person, Randy Minske. He's the only kid in class that no one payed any attention to.

He had brown curly hair, and had really bad body odor. All the kids say that he has lice. If someone happens to touch him, they would play the game, "Randy germs no returns," worst of all I heard he wore no underwear.

I looked over at him and he smiles, with snot running down his face. I turned around with a sick feeling in me. I felt like crying. I thought to myself I have to be his partner, of all people. Then Mrs. Washington said to get our coats and to get with your partner again, and she had to say the worst thing, "Hold hands with your partner, so you won't lost them." I thought, I wouldn't mind loosing him. I didn't want to hold hands with a known nose picker, Yuk!

We walked outside to the bus. It was cold out the air was really brisk. I could see my breath. I always like that, it was neat, but not now. I didn't care. I just put my hands in my pocket. I never did hold hands with him. We got on the bus. I sat in one seat and I made him sit in another.

Now, I didn't want to go and see the big, red, shiny trucks. I was just wishing the day was over. I sat there pouting with my arms crossed, the whole time, just gleeming out the window, watching the blurred figures go by.

Cathy

LESSON TWENTY: SELF-EVALUATION

Objective: The students will be able to

- Practice self-evaluation in Revision 2.

Procedure:

This lesson may take *one or two class periods,* depending upon how extensively the students are willing or able to revise.

I. **REVISING:** Ask the students to choose between Freewritings 8 and 9 for Revision 2.

II. Explain that the final draft of this writing will be published in a class booklet.

III. Point out that students should first be concerned with ideas and making their reader "see" in this revision. There will be time later to edit for spelling and punctuation.

IV. Distribute the accompanying **Self-Evaluation Checklist for Revision 2.** Encourage the students to work as long as necessary on their revision.

V. While the students work independently, move from student to student, reading passages, looking over self-evaluation sheets, and asking questions about their plans for the writing.

VI. Encourage the students to use plenty of time for this revision. Their experience with revision is limited, however, and many are used to simply recopying a first draft. With encouragement, they may be willing to explore more possibilities. (When the papers have been revised as much as possible, the students will share their writings aloud in peer conferences.)

VII. As you respond to the good parts of a writing, point out to students what devices they are using, so they can begin to use them consciously. For example: "Your use of *repetition* works well at this point," or "The use of *contrast* between the happy, opening scene and the sad ending is effective." Give honest praise.

Name _____ Date _____

2.3 Self-Evaluation Checklist for Revision 2

1. Do a general read through. Treat the writing as if it belongs to someone else.

2. Are you satisfied with the order and organization of your paper? _____

   _____

3. What parts of your writing no longer seem necessary? _____

   _____

   _____

4. What are the best parts of your writing? _____

   _____

   _____

5. What parts of your writing tell rather than show? _____

   _____

   _____

6. What new facts and details can you add? _____

   _____

   _____

7. Examine the beginning and end of the writing. Is each satisfactory? _____

   _____

   _____

8. What title do you plan to use? _____

9. When you have revised as much as possible, rewrite the piece, if necessary (This will not be your final draft, however.)

LESSON TWENTY-ONE: SMALL GROUPS

Objective: The students will be able to

- Share Revision 2 with other students in the small circle.

Procedure:

I. Hand out the accompanying Small-Group Information and the Responding in the Small Group. Students may respond orally to the writing of their peers. However, if this is their first experience in a small circle, it is useful to have students write their responses. (If so, you will need to have three to four times the usual number of copies of the second handout.) The written responses are given to the author at the end of the peer conference.

II. Thoroughly explain your expectations for the small-group activity. The primary goal is to help students become independent writers. Don't be discouraged if the first work in the small circle isn't completely successful. Peer editing is a skill students must practice to learn.

III. One good option is to rehearse (prior to class) a small group of students so they may model their responses for the whole class. Be sure they follow the accompanying format.

IV. Appoint students to small groups. Three or four students to a group is a good number. Select group members. Don't let students group themselves. Ideally, students in each group should complement each other's strengths and weaknesses. Also keep in mind different personality types in making the selections. Let a group work together for an entire revised paper, but it's not a good idea to assign permanent groups. (See Part One, Chapter Four.)

V. Ask all students to work on Revision 2 in a round-robin in the small circle:
   A. A writer begins by reading his or her writing aloud.
   B. The peer group fills out the entire evaluation sheet in writing.
   C. After everyone in the group has finished writing his or her responses to the paper, the author asks, "What do you like about my writing?"
   D. Using their written notes as a basis for their answers, every member of the small groups responds out loud to the author's question.
   E. After everyone has responded to question 1, the author asks question 2, "What questions do you have about my writing?"
   F. The peer group takes turns responding to question 2.
   G. The author asks question 3, "What suggestions do you have for making my writing better?"

H. The peer group responds.

I. The written editing responses are given to the author of the paper at the end of all discussion about the writing.

J. The group moves on to the next student's paper until everyone in the small group has shared a writing and received peer responses.

K. Small groups may not all finish at the same time. When a group has completed its work, members are expected to work quietly and independently on their own revisions.

VI. After all students have finished, give the author additional time to make further changes in their drafts, changes that may incorporate suggestions from their peers.

A word of encouragement: It takes time for students to learn to work together in groups. However, students who help others can better see what is needed in their own drafts. They become more skillful writers when they are encouraged to make decisions. Growth comes when problems are solved. It is worth the struggle.

Name _____   Date _____

2.4 Small-Group Information

DIRECTIONS FOR THE AUTHOR:

1. Don't apologize for the writing.
2. Read your draft out loud just as it's written on the paper.
3. Allow your peer members time to fill in their response sheets.
4. Ask question 1: *What do you like about my writing?* Listen to the responses of every person in the group.
5. Ask question 2: *What questions do you have about my writing?* Wait for everyone's response.
6. Ask question 3: *What suggestions do you have for making this writing better?* Expect a response from everyone.
7. Ask to have anything you don't understand clarified.
8. Thank the members of your group.

DIRECTIONS FOR SMALL GROUPS:

1. Each member is expected to bring a draft of his paper to class on the due date.
2. After being assigned to a group, move your desks quietly into a small circle.
3. Quickly decide who will read first.
4. Listen carefully as a draft is being read. When an author is reading, no one else should be talking.
5. Fill in the sheet **Responding in the Small Group** for the author.
6. When asked, respond to the author's questions out loud. Do not interrupt others.
7. Remember to be kind and helpful in your responses.
8. When all oral responses have been completed, give the author your sheet of written responses.
9. Go on to the next author, and repeat the process.
10. After every person in the group has read, and if the other peer groups have not completed their work, continue working quietly and independently on your own revisions.

Remember, the purpose of writing groups is not to attack, criticize, or concentrate on surface error. It is a time to be supportive and kind, to let the writer know that you hear what he or she is saying. The peer group is a time to tell the writer what you like or what interests you most.

Author's Name _____ Date _____

2.5 Responding in the Small Group

Editor's name _____

1. What do you like about the writing?

_____

_____

_____

_____

2. What questions do you have about the writing?

_____

_____

_____

_____

3. What suggestions do you have for making the writing better?

_____

_____

_____

_____

LESSON TWENTY-TWO: REVISING FOR ECONOMY

Objectives: The students will be able to

- Practice eliminating wordiness in writing.
- Practice revising for economy.
- Practice recognizing strong repetition.

Procedure:

  I. **REVISING:** Students have had little practice in revising for economy because traditional writing assignments have often stipulated a particular length.
   - A. To achieve a desired length, most students have learned to pad writings with unnecessary words.
   - B. Good writers understand that revision involves adding information as well as subtracting redundancies.

 II. Distribute the accompanying worksheets **Revising for Economy** and **Revising a Student Paper** to each student for practice in revising for economy. Explain, discuss and correct the first three exercises as a class after students have completed them independently.

III. Ask students to study the writing by Martin. They are to eliminate unnecessary words and repeated ideas wherever possible. (Using a writing by someone other than a student in the class frees them to be a bit more objective at this point in the workshop.) If you wish, display a transparency of the writing on an overhead and ask the entire class to discuss options for editing the paper.

 IV. Emphasize that strong repetition is a powerful writing technique. Have the students indicate where repetition might be preserved in Martin's paper.

  V. If time allows, ask students to look at their own Revision 2 to edit for economy.

2.6 Revising for Economy

Suppose your English teacher has assigned a composition. "Write 250 words about . . . ." Now, forty minutes later, you sit at your desk counting, 247, 248, 249. One word to go. You stare at the wall. Bite on your pencil. Finally, inspiration strikes! You grab your pen and stick another *and* into a sentence. Success!

A terrific writing! Right?

No.

Now that you've succeeded in putting words together effectively, the next step is to learn what words to take out. The first word to go is probably the extra *and* you inserted for padding.

Good writers revise their writing to eliminate unnecessary words, keeping only the best and essential. Good writing is economical.

The following sentences will help you practice for economy.

GET RID OF UNNECESSARY REPETITION:

For example: He repeated *again* . . . (omit "again")

Cross out all repeated words and ideas.

1. The sunset was orange in color.
2. The table was square in shape.
3. In my opinion, I think I have written well.
4. Her final conclusion was he should be given the prize.
5. If the girls cooperate together, they will finish the decorations.
6. Three round tennis balls rolled from the package.
7. As she lectured, the teacher referred back to her notes.
8. He looked at Mike. Mike was his brother.
9. My father subscribes to the *Tribune,* and he reads the *Tribune* every day.
10. Tom always tells me the truth, and he doesn't lie to me.
11. Jack is the best player on the team. He really is a great player.
12. Scott got a raise so he is making more money now.
13. Lisa is a talented pianist and really plays the piano well.
14. His radio doesn't work because it is broken.

GET RID OF EXCESS WORDS:

Sometimes we simply use too many words for the job. Although such padding may not be considered incorrect, it often clutters the sentences and prevents writers from expressing ideas clearly and concisely. For example: *The reason why* he didn't go to the dance *was* because he had no money. (Four words can be eliminated.)

Get rid of unnecessary words in the following sentences:

1. Kari was unhappy because of the fact that she had not been asked to the dance.
2. The point I would like to make is good writing is economical.
3. What I believe is that women should have the same rights as men.
4. What I mean is that Mom's ideas about keeping my room clean are not realistic.
5. We didn't hear a word on account of the fact it was noisy.
6. The reason why I want to get that job is because it pays well.
7. After the excitement, the fact was I couldn't fall asleep.
8. The thing that nobody could understand was Jane's attitude.
9. What I couldn't help noticing was how happy he looked.
10. Because of the fact that he knew the owner, John got the job.
11. All I wish is that I had gotten more sleep.
12. One thing I want is an extra day of vacation.

REDUCE CLAUSES TO SINGLE WORDS OR PREPOSITIONAL PHRASES:

For example: When the nights are clear, there may be frost.
Revised: On clear nights, there may be frost.

Revise the following sentences:

1. There were two students who were late for class.

2. Brad was a student who was shy and nervous.

3. When he was almost at the finish line, the runner collapsed.

4. Lori was chosen by a majority that was very small.

5. The girls who had run away were returned to their parents.

6. When the sun rises, the meadowlarks begin to sing.

7. I hoped to catch a bus which would take me downtown.

AVOID OVERUSING WORDS SUCH AS: *TYPE, SITUATION, FACTOR, KIND, ONE, ASPECT,* AND *AREA.*

For example: The story is about [the situation of] a girl speaking of her dreams.

2.6 (cont'd)

Revise the following sentences:

1. Her life was not a carefree one.

2. Jim is the type of a student who always loves a joke.

3. The student has problems in the area of mathematics.

4. Most people do not get the right kind of exercise.

Rewrite the following sentences, eliminating as many "I's" as possible:

1. Because I don't usually agree with Bill, I want to point out that I agree with him on this subject.

2. I had dolls that talked and cried and opened their eyes, but I never had a doll that I loved as much as I did Baby Hiccups.

3. I can remember vividly how I felt when I first drove the car alone.

4. I felt I was too ill to continue. I really thought I was going to pass out. I was scared because I was sure I would not be found until it was too late.

2.7 Revising a Student Paper

The following student writing is a good anecdote but far too wordy. Practice editing the paper. Eliminate unnecessary words and phrases and repeated ideas.

Mother hollered, "Come on everyone! It's time to eat!" We all rushed to the kitchen table to eat our supper. My father sat at the end of the kitchen table in his usual spot. My sisters and brother all sat down in their regular chairs. Since I was only four years old, I sat next to my mother. My mother always made sure that I would eat everything on my plate. Our supper that night was pretty basic. Mom had some toast, salad, and glorified rice as a side course. Our main course of the meal was Franco-American Ravioli. Mom like to make these, because they were easy to prepare.

Well, I watched my mother pile my plate up with food. She put a spoonful of glorified rice, a piece of toast, and a giant scoop of ravioli on my plate. I didn't get the salad because I never ate it. I started to eat my meal. I devoured the ravioli first. I loved the rich cheese and sauce. I enjoyed biting the ravioli in half and eating the meat inside. After I finished eating the ravioli, I ate my glorified rice and roast. I took a big drink of milk and was ready for more ravioli. I asked for some and again devoured everything. Everyone else was pretty full when Mom asked, "Would anyone care for any more ravioli?" I took another gulp of milk and said, "Uh huh." Well, mom emptied the pan of ravioli onto my plate. I kept on eating, and I ate everything.

I can't remember what I did that night after supper, but what I do remember is getting to sleep. I shared a bed with my brother. I was still really full from supper, and my brother was almost asleep. I can remember tossing and turning in my bed. I felt hot. I felt like a balloon with too much air. The last thing I remember is rolling over and saying, "Bud, I feel sick!" And I was—all over his face.

Today my brother and I laugh about this situation, but neither of us can look at, smell, or eat ravioli.

Martin

LESSON TWENTY-THREE: PROOFREADING

Objective: The students will be able to

- Practice proofreading skills.

Procedure:

This lesson may take *two class periods*.

REVISING: Editing for spelling and punctuation.

I. Place the following sentences on the blackboard and ask students to make suggestions for punctuating each in at least two different ways. Point out the significance of punctuation for meaning.

   A. These boys and girls are fine ladies and gentlemen.
      These, boys and girls, are fine ladies and gentlemen.
      These boys and girls are fine, ladies and gentlemen.
   B. She served tuna salad sandwiches cheese cake and tea.
      She served tuna salad sandwiches, cheese cake, and tea.
      She served tuna salad sandwiches, cheese, cake, and tea.
   C. Sara said the teacher is unhappy.
      Sara said, "The teacher is unhappy."
      "Sara," said the teacher, " is unhappy."
   D. Will you teach me how to cook Dad.
      Will you teach me how to cook, Dad?
      Will you teach me how to cook Dad?
   E. I saw a man eating shark.
      I saw a man-eating shark.
      I saw a man eating shark.

II. Hand out copies of the accompanying Student Writing Sample for Practice Editing.

   A. Give students time to edit independently.
   B. After students have had time to edit, discuss the paper and editing decisions with the class as a whole. (You may wish to use a transparency and an overhead projector.)

III. If the students need additional work with commas, collect sentences from the writing of your own students for a whole class discussion.

IV. Students will have a variety of editing problems, and many can be handled in brief teacher–student conferences. (Minilessons concentrating on one kind of error may be presented to groups of students or the entire class. Final papers at this point in the course will not be error free, but students do become more skillful editors as the workshop continues. A grammar book is a useful resource for these brief lessons.)

Name _____ Date _____

2.8 Student Writing Sample for Practice Editing

my sarah

I scrubbed the last of the smashed peas and dried on ketchup from her high chair sarah loved ketchip I smiled remembering the day Id put some on her hamberger when she wouldnt eat it then she wanted it on everything from sallmon to green beats she also managed to get it on her clothes face and high chair too I giggled remembering the sight she was when she was through I tossed the pine sol cleaning rag into the sinck after finishing the cleaning touches in the kitchen my fingers were wrinkled from the scalding water Id used to clean up as I walked toward the living room I heard the clattering of building blocks sarah sat on the plush brown carpet near the fireplace with her legs crossed in front of her molly her favorite rag doll was draped over her arm as she read to her the tales of winnie the poo i sunk down into the leather back recliner to relax it still smelled of armor all from its weekly cleaning sarah lifted her head and smiled at me my heart skipped a beat as i sat watching her play so contendly and carefully with molly she cradled her in her arms just like I did before putting her down for a knap I wondered silently if she knew how much I loved her after all I was only nanny sarah gently placed molly aside as she stook and walked toward me her small hands grasped my leg as she leaned her body forward and rested her head on my lap my fingers ran through her blond curls I smiled when I discovered a smashed pea that was buried beneath the surface of her winding curls she lifted her head and stared at me with a blank face do you need a snuggle I whispered having seen this expression before her eyes twinkled with glee and she nodded her head her curls bouncing with its motion I gathered her in my arms and her head fell to my shoulder thats when I knew ketchup wasnt all sarah loved

LESSON TWENTY-FOUR: POLISHING FOR PUBLICATION

Objective: The students will be able to

• Produce a final, polished writing for inclusion in a class booklet.

Procedure:

This lesson is likely to take at least *two class periods*.

   I. Announce a due date for the final copy of Revision 2 and insist that students meet this deadline in order to have all writings duplicated by the school's printing department.

  II. Give students plenty of time and encouragement to edit their final drafts independently.

 III. When the students have completed their independent editing, have them work in pairs to proofread one another's drafts. Hand out the accompanying checklist, **Proofreading a Final Draft.**

  IV. Read and discuss the checklist: Explain that as a writing nears completion, the author is concerned with editing for mechanical concerns such as spelling and punctuation. Because final drafts of these papers are to be published in a class booklet, the students will want to polish the final draft of Revision 2 as completely as possible.

   V. Require a neatly written, polished copy of Revision 2 for inclusion in the class booklet. Be clear about your final copy standards: Is the final draft to be written in ink? (If so, supply plenty of white correction fluid.) Is the paper to be unlined? Is the student to write on one side only? What kind of margins should the writer observe? (The left margin should be wide enough to staple the booklet.)

  VI. Remind students to give each writing a title. It may symbolize the meaning of the story, name a key element, or reflect a mood.

 VII. Ask for volunteers to design a book cover and table of contents.

Author _____ Date _____

Editor _____

2.9 Proofreading a Final Draft

Prepare your final draft for publication by editing it as carefully as possible. When you have questions, make use of helpful resources: dictionaries, an English handbook or grammar book, a classmate who is a skillful editor, or your teacher.

Editor   **Author**

_____   1. Are all the words spelled correctly?   _____

_____   2. Is all end punctuation correct?   _____

_____   3. Are words capitalized correctly?   _____

_____   4. Are commas where they belong?   _____

_____   5. Do all the verbs agree with their subjects?   _____

_____   6. Is the writing free of sentence fragments?   _____

_____   7. Are the paragraph indentions where they should
                be?   _____

_____   8. Is the writing economical?   _____

LESSON TWENTY-FIVE: PRACTICE IN RESPONDING

Objectives: The students will be able to

- Practice making revision suggestions.
- Understand papers often undergo several revisions.

Procedure:

I. Ask students to share a journal entry with the class and/or share one of your own. Remind students to consider using topics they have "found" in journal writing as an early draft for a more polished piece.

II. Provide further practice in responding to writing.
    A. Hand out copies of **Draft 1 of Jerry's Writing**.
    B. Have students work independently or, if you wish, assign students to groups and ask them to discuss the draft and report back with a group analysis.
    C. Have the students respond to the writing using the usual format:
        1. What do you like about Jerry's writing?
        2. What questions do you have about his writing?
        3. What suggestions do you have for making the writing better?

III. After responses have been made for the first draft, hand out **Draft 2 of Jerry's Writing**. (Students may assume that Jerry has considered their suggestions in making the new draft.)

IV. Have students again respond to the new draft (either in groups or individually).
    A. What do students like about this paper? (How has it improved?)
    B. Do they have questions?
    C. What suggestions would they make for further improvement?
        1. One question likely to arise is the language of the dialogue. Help students decide about its appropriateness to the writing. Does Billy's language show something about Billy's personality? Will members of the student audience be offended? What is your own reaction to explicit language in student writing?

Another option: Have students produce their own third draft of Jerry's writing.

Name _____ Date _____

2.10 Draft 1 of Jerry's Writing

1   The year was 1975; the season, winter; and the
2 grade school year, fourth grade. I was ten years old and a
3 fairly sizeable boy at the time. The only problem was that
4 there was another boy, a sixth grader to be exact, who was
5 bigger than I was and he decided that I was the perfect
6 specimen to beat up and pick on to show his friends he was
7 hot stuff. Being the person I was, I wouldn't stand for it
8 at first but after getting beaten up and thrown around
9 awhile, I soon realized I was no match for him. I was
10 scared!
11   The whole winter dragged on as a result of this fear.
12 Every lunch hour was wasted for my activities included
13 hiding under cars in hope that my adversary would not see
14 me. It got quite damp and cold just lying there, peering
15 through openings under the car. I was very lucky that
16 someone hadn't decided to drive somewhere for I would have
17 been flattened like a pancake. Nothing that but I probably
18 would've been killed.
19   The year was finally over and I knew I could breathe.
20 This sixth grader would be in high school and I wouldn't
21 have to see him for awhile.
22   Both he and I are much older now and every once in a
23 while I see him in the distance. Each times that happens,
24 I remember those days in fourth grade. I doubt if he
25 remembers what happened but then, he wasn't the one who
26 was scared.

                          Jerry

2.11 Draft 2 of Jerry's Writing

1   The year was 1975, the season: winter, and year in school, fourth grade. I

2 was ten years old and a fairly big kid at the time. School had been going well

3 until one day in November. It was from this day on, throughout the rest of the

4 school year, that I experienced something new in my life.

5   Billy, a sixth grader and a big bully in school, really had it in for me. I'm

6 not sure how it got started or why he chose me to push around, but he did and I

7 had quite a time trying to avoid him. Every day, in some way, he would get at

8 me. That was, of course, if I couldn't keep him from seeing me. I had just

9 wished once that I could overpower the creep. That might have made him

10 think twice on working me over.

11   All of the things I went through with him had the same tone or theme to

12 them; him being King Macho, and me, the one he rules over. One time I was

13 leaving the school on my lunch hour to try and find the rest of the gang. Well,

14 Billy saw me walking down the sidewalk. Keeping himself out of my sight, he

15 crept behind me. He was directly behind when he spoke.

16   "Hey, punk, I want you down on your knees when I'm around!" As I swung

17 around he kicked my legs out from under me. Collapsing to the ground, I lay

18 there, blood running from my hands and a bruise on my elbow. Getting to my

19 feet, I just looked at him.

20   "What's the matter?" he babbled, "can't you stay on your feet? Ahh, poor

21 baby! I think it's about time you eat some snow."

22   Instantly he shoved me to the ground. My face was now buried in snow.

23 With both hands clasped to my head, he rolled it vigorously, scraping and

24 clawing it, my face ripping with every movement in the ice chunks. The bell

25 rang. It was not until then that he finally quit. I just lay there. My face was a

26 mess but I didn't say anything. Returning to school, I finished the day out.

27   My hate for Billy became stronger with each day. I was going to stand up

28 to that sucker once and for all. After a week of persecution, my hate for him

29 was at a peak. I could take it no longer. The next day I saw Billy standing in

30 the hockey rink. Walking up, I waited for him to say just one word to me

31 knowing quite well that he would. He did, and that was all that I needed. My

32 first punch landed in his mouth. He didn't bulge. The second one went for his

33 stomach; NO EFFECT!!! I knew that I had made a mistake as I smashed into

34 the boards of the rink. He started towards me again, his eyes ablaise. I was

35 petrified! He was not five feet from me when one of his friends yelled, "Billy,

36 not now—a teacher's coming!" Backing off he grunted, 'You're safe for now,

37 you damn little shit. But you just wait until tomorrow."

38   I knew he meant it. What am I going to do? I thought to myself, I have

39 school for every day for the rest of the year. If he doesn't get me one day, he'll

40 get me another.

41   For the next day and the rest of the year, I began a daily routine of hiding

42 behind trees, snoebanks, under cars, and beneath bushes, any place I could

43 find that would keep me away from Billy's path for I was in constant fear of his

44 wrath. I got very lonely always hiding but I was too scared to do anything else.

45   The year was finally over and I had managed to escape from Billy's sight.

46 He would be going into seventh grade and a different school. I wouldn't have to

47 see him again for at least a couple of years.

48   Now, at 18, eight and a half years later, things have changed. Whenever I

49 see Billy, I vividly remember my ordeal in fourth grade. But the difference is

50 that I no longer have the hate I had for him. Besides, I doubt if Billy even

51 remembers those happenings. He wasn't the one who was scared.

LESSON TWENTY-SIX: PUBLISHING

Objective: The students will be able to

• Review and share the class publication.

If you plan to have each student read his or her final draft in the large circle, this lesson will take *several days*.

Procedure:

I. If possible, all final drafts of Revisions 2 will have been duplicated by this day. If not, schedule this activity for a later time.

II. Ideally, the school's printing center has assembled the class booklets. If not, have the students work together, assembling and stapling copies. (They may need a heavy-duty stapler.)

III. **PRESENTING** in the large circle:
   A. Arrange students in the large circle.
   B. Begin with large circle questions (see Part One, Chapter Four).
   C. Have the authors take turns reading their final drafts out loud. Have the student audience follow along in the booklets.
   D. Invite the author and students from the author's small group to make comments about the changes the writing has undergone from first to last draft.
   E. Additional questions for each author:
      1. What do you like best about your writing?
      2. What one thing will you do to improve your next writing?
      3. What kind of experimentation in writing would you like to try?

IV. Students may elect to send copies of the booklet to other classes, other subject area teachers, administrators, or family members.

V. Keep the original copies of Revision 2. (These will be used again in Lessons Thirty-three and Forty-three and included later in the students' personal booklets.) If grading is necessary, it should happen at this point and may reflect the writer's use of specific detail, economy, and appropriate use of punctuation. Another option is to assign a grade based on growth between Revision 1 and Revision 2.

unit 3

CREATING SETTING AND MOOD

Lessons Twenty-seven through Thirty-three require students to complete Freewritings 9, 10, and 11 and to again carry one writing through the entire process as Revision 3. Students practice visualization as a prewriting activity, work to create mood in their writing, and have the option of writing from a third-person point of view. Editing activities review the use of the thesaurus as an editing tool, emphasize the choice of powerful verbs, and offer practice in sentence combining.

LESSON TWENTY-SEVEN: SHOWING AN EMOTION

Objective: The students will be able to

- Practice showing rather than telling in Freewriting 9.

Procedure:

I. Distribute copies of the accompanying get-acquainted questions, **Do You Know the People in This Class?** Encourage students to move about the room to find the answers. These questions are a pleasant way to begin the period and to continue to build trust and friendship among the students. Compare and discuss student answers.

II. **PREWRITING:** Continue work with *showing* rather than telling.

A. Ask the students to define the word *emotion.*

B. Brainstorm with the students on the blackboard. Ask them to suggest as many words as possible which name emotions. A partial list might look like this:

rage	*boredom*	*grief*	*envy*	*love*
anxiety	*jealousy*	*hope*	*happiness*	*impatience*

C. Choose a type of person, for example, a *teen-age boy.*

D. Pick one word naming an emotion from the list, for example, *boredom.*

E. Ask students to help you brainstorm a list of actions a *bored teen-age boy* might exhibit in a classroom. A list might look like this:

bored   *teen-age boy*

> *walks slowly*
> *sighs*
> *slouches in desk*
> *fiddles with objects*
> *ignores school work*
> *sleeps*

F. Read the following sample writing aloud. Point out that the boy's actions *show* he is bored. The writer shows rather than tells.

The classroom bell had already rung when Jimmie plodded through the door. He moved heavily toward his desk, tossing a single tattered grammar book on the desk top. He sighed and lowered himself into his desk. He glanced around the room, pushed his glasses up his nose, then drummed the desk top with his fingertips. He thumbed through his book, fiddled with a nail clipper. Finally, he crossed his arms on the desk top, leaned forward, and put his fore-head on his arms.

    G. Have the students repeat the exercise independently.
        1. Choose one word naming an emotion and write it at the top of a sheet of paper.
        2. Identify a type of person (e.g., young girl, elderly matron) and write these words alongside the word naming the emotion.
        3. Brainstorm and list ways this person might behave while feeling this emotion.

III. **DRAFTING** Freewriting 9: A sample direction.

Look over your brainstorming list again. Now, *without naming the emotion,* write an eight- to ten-minute freewriting showing the actions and behavior of the person experiencing or feeling the emotion you have chosen. Show how this person would act.

IV. **EDITING AND PRESENTING:** Inform the students that once the writing is completed, and after they have edited briefly, they will be asked to read their drafts to the class.

    A. When the papers are read aloud, ask the class members to identify the emotion the author is showing.
    B. Again, remind students to keep this and all freewritings in their folders. Lesson Thirty in this unit will ask students to combine Freewritings 10 and 11 and develop it as Revision 3.

Name _____ Date _____

3.1 Do You Know the People in this Class?

Move around the room, talking with one another to find the answers.

1. Find the name of someone in this class with the same shoe size as yours. _____

2. Find the name of someone in this class who has been to a major league baseball game. _____

3. Find the name of someone in this class who has traveled outside the continental United States. _____

4. Find someone who has a funny middle name. _____

5. Find someone whose favorite food is liver. _____

6. Find someone who has written more than the required number of journal entries. _____

7. Find someone who walked to school this morning. _____

8. Find someone who has a living grandparent at least eighty years old. _____

9. Find someone who had tomato juice for breakfast this morning. _____

10. Find someone who owns an unusual pet. _____

    What is it? _____

LESSON TWENTY-EIGHT: VISUALIZING

Objective: The students will be able to

• Write freely about an emotion in Freewriting 10.

Procedure:

I. PREWRITING

A. Read the following samples of student writing to the class:

A FRIGHTENING MEMORY

It will soon be 2:30 P.M., August 7th. I am driving, and Brian is sleeping in the seat next to me. We are on our way from Duluth to Bemidji, traveling east on County Road 86, ten miles from Park Rapids.

Ahead, out of the watery mirage on the road, a semi-truck approaches. All of a sudden another car appears, a white, two-door. It has passed the semi and is coming toward us in our lane.

I freeze, turning the steering wheel toward the right-hand ditch. As if mimicing my moves, the white car moves in the same direction. There is a blur of flying glass and corn stalks. Batteries explode. Tires pop off. It ends with a loud thud. Our car is facing north in the middle of the highway. I can hear a far-away siren.

John

A HAPPY MEMORY

As my foot presses on the gas pedal, the old yellow Dodge shivers and hums more loudly. I glance down at the speedometer; the thin red needle creeps up to 60, then a bit beyond. "Well, I guess I'm not too much of a criminal," I excuse myself. I have been away from home for a whole year, as an exchange student in Norway, and my foot is tapping along with the radio as I wish away these last twenty miles.

Dad's question from the back seat startles me, "Is it starting to look familiar now?"

I sigh, "Uh-huh," and I can't keep from smiling.

We pass Susie's house. I look searchingly down the driveway, as if in that second I'll see her come running to meet me. My disappointed eyes return to the highway. As we near Bemidji, something wraps around my heart and lungs. It's hard to breathe. That same thing plays tricks on my eyes. I blink to see. The sunlight hitting the dark, blue water of Lake Bemidji creates countless, tiny flashes of light. The ferris wheel of the lakeside amusement park moves in its circle. Herb's Popcorn wagon stands red and shiny with its green and white awning lowered in defense of the sun. At the stoplight, the red

124

takes one minute and fifteen seconds to change. Groaning, I rest my chin on a sweaty left hand. Oh—green! The car chugs to motion again. As we continue up Bemidji Avenue, I think, "What? No brass band? No banner welcoming me home?" Chuckling out loud, I turn the corner onto Highway Two West. We drive the rest of the way in silence except for Mom's occasional comments about the changing state of the trees along Irving Avenue.

As we pull into the driveway, rock and gravel crunch beneath the tires. There's Poo dog flopped in the shade of the porch. Rising stiffly, she ambles over and sniffs this stranger she hasn't seen in a year. She's still as huggable as ever. My brother isn't, but I squeeze him a good one, anyway.

Banging through the front door, I laugh as I run up to my room, taking the steps two at a time.

Karin

A SAD MEMORY

My mother and I had a great relationship. We suffered hard times, like when my dad died, and we smiled through the happy ones, like the time we went to Maine on vacation. My mother and I went almost everywhere together. We would go to the movies, shopping, and on special trips. Janie, Sharon and Shirley were her friends, but I also shared that relationship just the way she shared mine with Carrie, Teresa, and Lisa.

On the day she died, I felt as though I couldn't go on. It was a shock, because when she went into the hospital for the hysterectomy, she was laughing and smiling and feeling no pain at all. It wasn't the operation that turned bad. She had a stroke after surgery. My mother went into the hospital on Wednesday and died on Sunday.

When I first realized that my mother wasn't going to make it, I was sitting in the waiting room in St. Luke's hospital in Duluth. I knew by the way the doctor looked at me and said, "Diane, would you like to go for a short walk with me?" that there was something wrong. When he told me "Diane, I'm sorry, but we have done everything we can do. I'm really sorry," I started to cry. Then I grabbed him saying, "It's not fair. Please don't let her die. She is all I got. Please!"

Diane

B. Explain that the authors of the sample writings were writing about feelings and emotions: happy, scary, and sad.
C. Ask the students to write the headings: happy, scary, and sad on the top of their own papers.
D. Have them brainstorm and list beneath these headings possible

topics from their own experiences for each category. Encourage them to make the longest list possible.

   E. Have students choose one topic that holds the most possibilities for a freewriting.

   F. **VISUALIZATION EXERCISE** for Drafting Freewriting 10: After students have zeroed in on one idea, give the following directions:

I'm going to ask you to travel in time. Relax your body, make yourself comfortable in your desk, put down your pen or pencil, and close your eyes. Let my voice put pictures in your mind. We're going to return to a past time, the time of the memory you have picked to write about, a happy or sad or scary time. Keep your eyes closed and see the memory again in your mind. If you were young at the time of this memory, shrink yourself down to the size you were then. Where are you? What do you see? What colors do you notice? What do you smell? What do you hear? Are you outside? What is the weather like? If you're inside, look around the room. What do you see? What are the physical props of the scene? Are other people present? Who? What are they doing? Now I want you to watch yourself. What are you doing? Watch yourself move through the scene. Look at this memory for as long as you'd like, and when you are ready, pick up your pen or pencil and freewrite for as long as possible about what you saw as you visited your memory. You'll have until the end of the class period to write down as much as you possibly can.

II. **DRAFTING:** Encourage the students to use all the remaining class time for Freewriting 10.

LESSON TWENTY-NINE: SETTING AND MOOD

Objectives: The students will be able to

- Understand *setting* and *mood*.
- Brainstorm for details that create a setting and mood in their own writings.
- Complete Freewriting 11.

Procedure:

This lesson will take *two class periods*.

DAY ONE

1. Ask students to reread their Freewritings 10 from the previous lesson.
2. Define the term *mood*.
   a. What does it mean to be in a *good mood* or a *bad mood*? Are there other moods?
   b. Explain that writers are often concerned with creating a mood or a feeling or tone for their writings.
   c. Point out that the mood of a writing may change from the beginning to the end of a story. This contrast can be effective.
3. Write several of the following sentences on the blackboard or display them on the overhead projector. Explain that they come from separate writings.
   a. *The dead rabbit's blood dripped into the sink.*
   b. *I could hear the loons singing as water lapped against the dock.*
   c. *The children walked past an untrimmed hedge and a bed of snapdragons.*
   d. *Lightning flashed, and the curtains at the open window danced frantically.*
   e. *The hot sun above the avocado tree watches our whispered lies crackle on the cement.*
4. Ask the students to speculate about the mood or feeling of the entire piece of writing from which each sentence is taken. Ask them to pick words or details from each sentence which contribute to a particular mood.
5. Explain that the emotional reaction they have had to each sentence is something the author desires. A writer seeks to create a mood and deliberately chooses and inserts details to accomplish this.
6. Hand out the accompanying brainstorming worksheet, **Creating Setting and Mood**.
7. Read and explain the worksheet and give the students time to complete it independently. Offer individual help to those who need it.

8. **DRAFTING** Freewriting 11: Have the students use their brainstormed material from the worksheet to write a new beginning or introduction (several paragraphs) for Freewriting 10. Ask them to describe a setting and create a mood for their story. Some teachers encourage their students to invent additional information. If you are comfortable with this mixing of fiction and nonfiction, encourage your students to create new facts or details if these will add to the mood they wish to create.

9. This activity is likely to take an entire class period. If there is time, ask volunteers to read their new, introductory paragraph aloud.

DAY TWO

1. On the second day of this lesson, give students time to combine Freewritings 10 and 11 in any way necessary to make a more complete writing.

2. Students should understand they are beginning Revision 3 which will continue to undergo revision and ultimately will be shared with the whole class in the large circle.

3. Encourage students to insert new details throughout the entire writing which will contribute to its mood and to delete any unnecessary details which draw attention away from it. You may wish to point out that the initial mood of a writing may change, and this contrast can be effective.

Another option: This is an ideal time to introduce writing from another point of view. Up to this point in the workshop, the students are likely to have written only in first person. Consider encouraging those students who need a challenge to write this piece in the third person.

Name _____ Date _____

3.2 Creating Setting and Mood

Readers respond emotionally to good writing. The term *mood* has to do with the emotional effect of a writing. How do you want your reader to respond to your Freewriting 10, for example? Do you want him or her to smile, to feel sad, to be afraid? (Circle one.) Once you have made this decision about a writing, every choice you make as a writer will help you create this mood. The mood of a writing may change from the beginning to the end of a piece. This contrast can be effective.

A writer also creates a setting for a story. The term *setting* has to do with when and where a story is happening, a sense of place and time. Good writers have the ability to create a setting an audience will believe.

Creating both setting and mood is like setting a stage for a play. For this brainstorming exercise, suppose a movie is going to be made of your Freewriting 10, and you have been hired to be in charge of the set. (You are free to invent any new details you wish.) Answer the following questions concerning the opening scene and setting of your movie:

1. What are the colors of the scene? _____

_____

2. What do you want the audience to see first? _____

_____

3. What do you want the audience to hear? _____

_____

4. What do you want the audience to smell? _____

5. What is the weather and season of this scene? _____

_____

6. What is the time of day? _____ How will the audience know?

_____

7. List some props you want to place in the scene and describe each in a word or two:

_____   _____

_____   _____

_____   _____

8. Suppose a character enters the scene. Name and describe the character.

_____

_____

9. What is the character feeling? _____ How will the audience know?

_____

_____

_____

_____

LESSON THIRTY: CHOOSING THE BEST WORD

Objective: The students will be able to

• Use a thesaurus in editing for word choices.

Procedure:

I. Write the following sentences on the blackboard and ask students to translate each common cliche. Ideally, they will find the task difficult. Explain that big words frequently interfere with communication.

    A. *It's not feasible for mendicants to be indicators of preference.* (Beggars can't be choosers.)

    B. *Abstain from becoming lachrymose due to the scattering of lacteal fluid.* (Don't cry over spilt milk.)

    C. *The individual of the class Aves arriving prior to the appointed time seizes the invertebrate animals of the phylum Vermes.* (The early bird catches the worm.)

II. Give each student a copy of a thesaurus and explain its format.

III. Distribute the worksheet, **Choosing the Right Word**, and have the students complete the thesaurus exercise. The following are possible solutions to the exercise:

    A. omitting "o's": *Many years in the past, there were three bears living in a snug dwelling in the timber.*

    B. omitting "e's": *Long ago, a trio of bruins did subsist in a snug barrack in a stand of saplings.*

IV. You may wish to introduce an additional activity: Have students write sentences which make sense, using all the letters of the alphabet. For a further challenge, limit the sentences to fifty letters.

V. If there is time, an additional exercise, **Choosing Precise Adjectives,** provides further practice.

Name _____ Date _____

3.3 Choosing the RIGHT Word

People write to communicate, and when they write, there is no law that says writers must use big words. However, many people do try to use fancy words simply because they think these make their writing sound important and impressive. Two things that can keep writing from being clear to an audience are big words, which are usually too abstract to make pictures in the mind, and long sentences, which tax the memory. If, for example, someone asked you for a "juxtaposition of two oracularous muscles in a state of contraction," would you know you've been asked for a kiss? If you asked your parents for a raise in allowance and your father said, "Your unflagging requests for greater remuneration are totally unrealistic, and extenuating circumstances coerce me to preclude you from such extravagance," would you get it?

Big words can bog the reader down, forcing him or her to reread three or four times to make out what they mean. A sound rule to follow:

Use small, familiar words where you can; if a long word says just what you want to say, don't be afraid to use it.

Rather than deliberately choosing short or long words, a writer searches to find exactly the *right* words. One of the most helpful revision tools a writer has is a thesaurus, a reference book which presents a large number of synonyms or near synonyms for words. The following exercise is designed to give you more practice in using a thesaurus:

Remember the familiar story, "Once upon a time there were three bears who lived in a cozy cottage in a forest"?

1. For fun, rewrite this opening sentence without using any words that contain the letter "o." You'll have to make some substitutions, but the idea is to come up with a sentence that means the same as the original. Use the thesaurus for alternative words if you get stuck.

   _____

   _____

2. Now try it again, omitting any words with the letter "e."

   _____

   _____

Adapted from "Omit-It," by Ron Prahl, *Writing!* (January 1985), Curriculum Innovations Inc. Special permission granted by Field Publications.

Name _____ Date _____

3.4 Choosing Precise Adjectives

It was a *nice* day, and I was having *great* fun when I met this *interesting* girl who had a *super* smile and *terrific* car. It turned out to be an *amazing* day.

Sometimes students believe that good writing requires a long string of adjectives. No! Good writing can be made better with adjectives that create pictures in the reader's head. The words *underlined* above are simply filler. Does the word *nice*, for example, give the reader a picture of the day? Words like *nice, great, terrific*, and *amazing* are powerless adjectives and simply take up space in a writing. There are, however, some ways to use adjectives powerfully.

1. Don't use more adjectives than you need. Choose the best one.
2. Avoid vague words like *nice, awful, terrific, great, wonderful, awesome,* or *excellent.*
3. Avoid vague descriptions like *big, small, old,* or *new.*
4. Get rid of words that intensify adjectives like *very* or *really.* For example, "He is very concerned about you" is *less* forceful than "He is concerned about you."

Substitute more precise adjectives for the underlined words in the following sentences or rewrite the entire sentence.

1. You owe me <u>some</u> money.

2. Don't eat that <u>awful</u> food.

3. She had <u>terrific</u> fingernails.

4. My <u>old</u> car is unsafe.

5. I like her <u>great</u> haircut.

6. His <u>weird</u> underwear kept him from freezing.

7. That's an <u>interesting</u> idea.

LESSON THIRTY-ONE: CHOOSING STRONG VERBS

Objective: The students will be able to

- Substitute lively verbs for bland verbs.

Procedure:

I. Ask the students to complete the accompanying worksheet, **Verbs Are Some of the Most Important Words a Writer Chooses.**
   A. Poor verbs lack the power to create pictures.
   B. Poor verbs contribute to wordiness.

II. Discuss the completed worksheets:
    Some possible answers:

A.	waddled	C.	saw	D.	bolted
	tiptoed		slice		crashed
	strolled		gash		darted
	stomped		slit		fluttered
			chop		
B.	battled		nick		
	scuffled		whittle		

III. Have the students examine the verbs in their own Revision 3.
     A. Circle all verbs.
     B. Substitute better verbs when possible.
     C. Use a thesaurus if necessary.

IV. Instruct the students to use the remainder of the class period for revision while you confer individually with students. (Mechanical correctness is not yet a major concern.)

© 1990 by The Center for Applied Research in Education

Name _____ Date _____

3.5 Verbs are Some of the Most Important Words A Writer Chooses

Worn-out verbs can weaken sentences. Some of the more common are *do, give, get, have, hold, make, put,* and *take.* The following is an example of this type of writing:

My teacher is in the habit of being late, but on Thursday he got to our class on time. After making a diagram on the board and putting the labels on each part I saw him give a look out the window and then he took his leave of the astonished class.

Without the overworked verbs, the writing gains power and becomes more economical.

My teacher habitually *arrives* late, but on Thursday he *strode* into our class on time. After *diagramming* on the board and *labeling* each part, he *glanced* out the window and *deserted* the astonished class.

List powerful verbs for each sentence. Notice how the meaning changes with the choice of each verb. (Use a thesaurus, if necessary.)

1. The blonde girl *walked* down the steps.

   _____   (Make her heavy.)
   _____   (Make her shy.)
   _____   (Make her carefree.)
   _____   (Make her angry.)

2. Two boys *fought* in the hallway.

   _____   (Suggest anger.)
   _____   (Suggest playfulness.)

3. He used a knife to *cut* it.

   _____
   _____
   _____
   _____
   _____

4. The animal *came* out of the woods.

   _____
   _____

LESSON THIRTY-TWO: SELF-EVALUATION

Objective: The students will be able to

- Begin Revision 3 using a self-evaluation checklist.

Procedure:

I. Hand out **Self-Evaluation Checklist for Revision 3**.

II. Give students as much time as necessary to complete their self-evaluations and to revise their writings as completely as possible. The students will share their drafts with their peers in the small circle in Lesson Thirty-three. Also use this time for work with individual students.

Name _____   Date _____

3.6 Self-Evaluation Checklist for Revision 3

Avoid the old "recopy and turn in" approach to revision. Few pieces of writing are ever complete and polished in the first drafts. Take time for careful revision. Consider these questions as you work with Revision 3.

1. What is my purpose for this piece? _____

   _____

2. Have I shown my reader enough? _____

   _____

3. What mood am I creating at the beginning of the piece? _____

   _____

   Does the mood change as the piece continues? _____ If so, how? _____

   _____

4. Do all the facts, specific words, and details contribute to this mood? _____

   _____ Can I add more? _____

   _____

5. The best part(s) of my paper is (are) _____

   _____

   _____

6. The part(s) of my paper which need more work is (are) _____

   _____

   _____

7. Have I avoided cliches? _____

8. Have I avoided wordiness? _____

9. Have I chosen the best verbs and adjectives? _____

LESSON THIRTY-THREE: REVISION

Objectives: The students will be able to

- Completely polish and edit Revision 3.
- Analyze Revisions 1–3.

Procedure:

This lesson may take *seven to eight class periods.*

I. Decide if Revision 3 is to be completely polished and edited. If so, the following schedule is provided as a guide:

Day One:	Students hold peer conferences. (See Lesson Twenty-one.)
Day Two:	Students continue to work on Revision 3, taking into account the comments from their peers in the small circle and comments from you in student–teacher conferences.
Day Three:	If it is helpful at this point, distribute **Practice in Sentence Combining**. After completing the exercises, ask students to apply the concept to their own revision.
Days Four and Five:	Students complete their revisions, and, when ready, work in pairs or confer with the teacher to edit for mechanical correctness.
Day Six:	A final, polished draft is completed.
Days Seven and Eight:	Final drafts are read aloud in the large circle. Papers are collected and saved for Lesson Forty-three and for publication in a booklet in Unit Ten. Grading, if necessary, is done at this time and should reflect the student's ability to create mood and make specific word choices.

II. Student–teacher conferences: You may wish to conduct individual conferences with the students at the completion of Revision 3. If so, the accompanying handout, **Student Analysis of Revisions 1–3**, is included as an aid on which to base your conferences. Lesson Forty-three in Unit Six suggests conferences based on Revisions 1–5.

3.7 Practice in Sentence Combining

Another approach to revision has to do with combining sentences. Some writers edit by combining short sentences into longer ones. Does that mean that short sentences are bad? Not at all! But sometimes longer, more complex sentences best express what you want to say. Below are groups of short sentences. Practice combining each group into one or two sentences.

1. Sam was a musician.
   He was a vocalist.
   He sang with a group called "The Drones."
   He was not happy.
   He decided to do something about it.
   He enrolled at the university.
   He took preveterinary classes.

2. Chad lives in a small house.
   His room is in the basement.
   No one else in his family will go there.
   Dirty socks litter the floor.
   Old magazines are stuffed under the bed.
   Empty milk glasses and pizza crusts cover a nightstand.
   The room smells moldy.

3. The Hansons own a cat.
   Her name is Roo.
   It is short for Kangaroo.
   She teases the sheepdog.
   Its name is Muffin.
   She steals his food.
   She hides beneath the furniture.

4. Mrs. Hanson decided to cook a meal.
   She selected spaghetti and meatballs.
   The day before she had problems at her office.
   She is a lawyer.
   She thought about the problems as she cooked.
   The spaghetti burned.
   The family went out to eat.

Name _____ Date _____

3.8 Student Analysis of Revisions 1–3

Analyze your writings:

Revision 1   Strengths: _____

_____

Weaknesses: _____

_____

Revision 2   Strengths: _____

_____

Weaknesses: _____

_____

Revision 3   Strengths: _____

_____

Weaknesses: _____

_____

Which writing do you like best? _____ Why? _____

_____

What do you plan to work on in your next paper? _____

_____

What other experiences in writing would you like to have? _____

_____

What grade do you believe you have earned at this point? _____ Explain:

_____

_____

unit 4

USING DIRECT DIALOGUE

Lessons Thirty-four through Thirty-seven introduce students to direct dialogue. Students produce a dialogue (Revision 4) which may be presented before the whole class or polished as a radio play.

LESSON THIRTY-FOUR: DIALOGUE

Objective: The students will be able to

• Practice writing dialogue.

Procedure:

    I. Have each student write three statements expressing a feeling.
        A. You may give examples such as:
            1. *"I'm tired. I stayed up late reading."*
            2. *"It's only 9:00 A.M., and I'm hungry."*
            3. *"I itch from the prickles of the cactus plant I carried to school this morning."*
        B. Direct the students to leave spaces between their original three sentences so that additional material may be inserted.

   II. After all three sentences have been completed, ask the students to write a reply to each of their original three statements from someone else's point of view. For example, a student might reply to item 3 in the sample sentences this way: *"Geez, I didn't even notice that stupid plant three feet from me. Why didja bring a plant to school anyway?"*

  III. Ask the students to write a third response to each of the original statements from the point of view of a third speaker (or inanimate object). For example, the plant might answer: *"Oh my, I'm tired of being jiggled around. I'm still shaking from that ride. And now you've stuck me on a bookcase alongside a fake plastic plant with dusty leaves. I'd rather be by a warm window."*

  IV. After the students have finished writing, call on volunteers to read one of their three brief dialogues.

   V. Next, arrange the students in pairs. Ask each pair to draw one slip from the writing options listed on the following page. (These may be reproduced, cut apart, and placed in a container.)

  VI. Explain to the paired students:
        A. You are to work together to write one dialogue on one sheet of paper.
        B. You are each to become one of the two characters listed on your slip. Decide between yourselves which role each of you will take.
        C. One of you will begin by writing a statement from your character's point of view at the top of the paper.
        D. Pass the paper to your partner and let him or her reply in writing from his or her own character's point of view.
        E. Continue writing in this manner until you arrive at some kind of conclusion.

    VII. After about ten minutes, ask the pairs to edit their dialogues in any way necessary to read them to the class.

    VIII. Call on the pairs to read aloud. (This is simply a practice and papers need not be collected or recorded.)

Name _____ Date _____

Character Combinations for Dialogue Exercise

1. ninth grade boy his sister	8. a racoon a skunk
2. middle-aged man his 98-year-old father	9. a math teacher a girl student
3. a physical education teacher eleventh grade boy	10. a cafeteria worker a boy student
4. mother her 16-year-old son	11. janitor senior boy
5. two girls, age 9	12. two grandmothers
6. two boys, age 9	13. two grandfathers
7. father his 17-year-old son	14. a fast-food worker a teenage girl

LESSON THIRTY-FIVE: EXTENDED DIALOGUE

Objective: The students will be able to

- Write an extended dialogue as Freewriting 12.

Procedure:

I. Hand out the accompanying **Sample of Indirect Dialogue** and ask the students to convert it to direct dialogue.

   A. Explain the difference between indirect and direct dialogue (the latter uses the exact words of a speaker).

   B. When students have completed the exercise, ask for volunteers to read several versions. (The correct use of quotation marks will be discussed in Lesson Thirty-six.)

II. Read and discuss the accompanying **Stories Using Direct Dialogue.** You may wish to distribute copies to each student or display the writings on the overhead projector.

III. Brainstorm with the students on the blackboard about ideas for possibilities for characters and stories to be told in dialogue. (Conversations between children and relatives, brothers and sisters, parents or grandparents; conversations in the principal's office, the school halls, or at work.)

   A. Put an example of a set situation on the blackboard, for example, *four boys riding in a car.* Brainstorm all the different possibilities. Where are they going? Why? What if it's *two boys and two girls* or *four girls*? What if they're *walking,* or *running,* or *riding bicycles*?

   B. Help the students visualize potential story lines and involve the class in the fun of creating actual stories. A brainstorming format for the blackboard might look like this:

Who?	Where?	What?
four girls	in a car	going to school
four boys	riding bus	going to movie
two boys, two girls	riding bikes	going to beach
three boys and dog	walking	going to dance
senior citizens	cross country	going "cruising"

IV. Have the students brainstorm independently for a story idea.

   A. Pick and define two or three characters.

   B. What are the people doing? Suppose two brothers are at the police station. Why are they there? Another brainstorming list might look like this:

        arrested
        pick up father
        report theft
        sell tickets
        pay a fine
        visit a friend

V. **DRAFTING** Freewriting 12: A sample direction.

After you have determined who your speakers are and what is happening, use the remainder of the period to write a brief story primarily in dialogue.

VI. Encourage students to use the remainder of the class period for their writing. If someone finishes early, consult with her individually.

Adapted from "Starting Stories—They're Everywhere," Daniel Gabriel, 1987, used by permission

4.1 Sample of Indirect Dialogue

Sharon said that she was tired of the way she was leading her life. Todd expressed surprise. Sharon explained that she wanted to do something about her boring existence. Again, Todd responded in a surprised manner. Sharon said that she wanted to join the service to see the world and learn a skill. Todd was shocked. Sharon said that when she was done she would be a better person. Todd began to change his mind and understand her point of view.

This paragraph is written in indirect dialogue. In the space provided, convert it into direct dialogue (the exact words of the speakers).

_____

_____

_____

_____

_____

_____

_____

_____

_____

_____

_____

_____

4.2 Stories Using Direct Dialogue

FRIDAY NIGHT

"Hi, Dad, this is Martin."

"Where are you?"

"I'm on break from play practice. We are going to be practicing late tonight. The roads are bad, so I'm going to stay in town at Clint's tonight. O.K.?"

"Just a minute. . . . Carol, Martin wants to stay in town tonight.

"No! Tell him to come home."

"Your mother said that . . . ."

"I heard what she said. Let me talk to her."

"O.K."

"I said, 'Come home!' You don't have any clean clothes for play practice tomorrow. So just come home."

"I can wear something of Clint's. Mom, the roads are bad. I have play practice tomorrow morning. It is so stupid! I'm going to stay in town, O.K.?

"Well, I don't know . . . ."

"Mother! I am eighteen years old! I'm staying in town. O.K.?"

"Make sure you wear clean clothes."

"Sure, Mom. Bye."

"Be careful driving."

"O.K. Bye."

"Make sure you get up in the morning."

"Ya. Bye."

(Martin walks to a car full of kids.)

"Let's go! I told her that I have play practice late tonight, and that I am going to stay at my brother's."

Sam

THE HOME BEAUTY SHOP

"Oh my gosh!"

"What's wrong?"

"Nothing."

"Let me look."

"Not until it's done."

"How much longer?"

4.2 (cont'd)

"Not long now."
"What's it like?"
"It's pink going to orange."
"What! Let me look."
"Not until it's done."
"Hurry up."
"Look at it this way. It could be worse."
"How much worse?"
"It looks fine. We can always change it back."
"Let me look!"
"I'll dry it and style it first to take some of the shock away."
"Hurry up!"
"It could be worse."
"Shut up."
"All right. I'm done. You can look."
"Oh, my gosh. It's orange."
"It isn't that bad."
"It's orange. My hair is orange!"
"Oh, shut up."

Lori

LESSON THIRTY-SIX: PUNCTUATING DIRECT DIALOGUE

Objectives: The students will be able to

- Review rules for punctuating dialogue.
- Find a variety of dialogue tags.
- Begin Revision 4.

Procedure:

I. Distribute and discuss the accompanying sheet, **Review of Rules for Quotation Marks**.

II. Distribute a novel or a short story anthology to the class. Have the students study an author's use of direct dialogue. Comment on paragraphing and dialogue tags.

III. Hand out the accompanying worksheet, **Dialogue Tags**. Have the students do the exercises and discuss them.

Additional synonyms for said:
added, admitted, advised, agreed, announced, argued, bantered, claimed, commented, complained, confided, denied, fumed, giggled, grinned, instructed, laughed, mentioned, mused, noted, ordered, pleaded, prompted, quipped, reassured, repeated, retorted, scoffed, scolded, snapped, sneered, sputtered, stormed, urged, uttered, vowed, warned

Some possible answers:

1. insisted	2. proclaimed	3. droned	4. whispered	5. smiled
lectured	bragged	proclaimed	lisped	grinned
ordered	exclaimed	announced	drawled	confided

IV. **REVISING:** Ask the students to begin Revision 4, based on Freewriting 12. If you plan to have the students present their final draft to the whole class, be sure the students understand this. You may give them additional time to involve other classmates in their presentation. You may also wish to point out the following:

A. One speaker may dominate a conversation.
B. People often interrupt one another.
C. People don't always speak in complete sentences.
D. Different types of people have different speech characteristics. For example, a judge will speak differently than a criminal, a hockey coach will speak differently than a third grade teacher. Direct dialogue shows the reader something about a speaker and his or her personality.

Name _____ Date _____

4.3 Review of Rules for Quotation Marks

1. If you aren't using a person's exact words, don't use quotation marks.

   He told us he'd probably be here later.

2. If the person's words ask a question, state a command, or make a statement, place the appropriate punctuation inside the second quotation mark.

   She asked, "Why does this seem so difficult?"
   "Why does this seem so difficult?" she asked.
   "This is hard," she said.

3. When a person's sentence is interrupted with a dialogue tag (he said, she said), place a comma and quotation mark before and after the tag.

   "Stop it," he snarled, "before I really get angry."

4. If a statement ends before the dialogue tag, place a comma and quotation mark after the statement and a period after the tag.

   "Stop it," he snarled. "If you don't want trouble, stop it!"

5. If the sentence is a question, but the quotation is not, place the question mark outside the quotation marks.

   Didn't she say, "Forget it"?

6. If you use a semicolon which is not a part of the quotation, place it outside the quotation marks.

   Dad said, "I'll be home by six"; unfortunately, he had car trouble.

7. Begin a new paragraph each time the speaker changes.

8. If you quote one person for more than two paragraphs, use quotation marks at the start of each paragraph and at the end of the last paragraph.

Name _____ Date _____

4.4 Dialogue Tags

Ann is revising her writing. She would like to find synonyms to substitute occasionally for "she said" and "he said." In your thesaurus, check all entries under *say* and *said* and see if you can find substitute words that might be helpful.

_____   _____   _____

_____   _____   _____

_____   _____   _____

_____   _____   _____

_____   _____   _____

Dialogue tags: List at least three good verbs which would be appropriate for the following.

1. "Come right away," _____ mother. "Your supper is getting cold."

   _____

   _____

2. "I have wonderful news!" _____ the teacher as he rushed into the classroom.

   _____

   _____

3. "My fellow Americans," the candidate _____, "I come before you today to ask for your vote."

   _____,

   _____,

4. Sandy smiled flirtatiously at Tim and _____, "How do I look?"

   _____,

   _____,

5. "You are such a nice person," _____ Tom, "I just know you will help me."

   _____

   _____

LESSON THIRTY-SEVEN: REVISING

Objectives: The students will be able to

- Complete Revision 4.
- Present the revision to the whole class.

Procedure:

This lesson may take *two class periods*.

DAY ONE

1. Give students time to complete their final drafts of Revision 4.
2. Encourage students to work in pairs to edit for use of quotation marks.

DAY TWO

3. When the final, polished draft is completed, allow students to ask other class members to take speaking parts in order to present the dialogues to the entire class. Give students time to practice their presentations.
4. Ask students taking part in reading each dialogue to stand in front of the class to make their presentations.
5. Collect the final drafts and save them for Lesson Forty-three and publication in a personal booklet. If grading is necessary, do it at this point.

Some other options: You may wish to expand this assignment. For example, you could appoint a board of editors to select the strongest dialogues. The stories could be combined as a series of short radio plays. Student groups can polish, rehearse, and tape record the stories. They may also write original commercials. A final tape can be played for the whole class or exchanged with another writing class. The script may also be typed, illustrated, and presented to another class or the school library. In this case, you may decide to have students use script form rather than quotation marks. Stage directions will also become a consideration.

SHAPING A WRITING

Lessons Thirty-eight through Forty-two allow students to take Freewriting 13 through the entire writing process (Revision 5). New editing concerns have to do with the shape or organization of a writing and emphasize effective beginnings and endings.

Lessons Forty-three and Forty-four encourage self-evaluation on the part of the students and allow time for student-teacher conferences. Students are encouraged to reevaluate a previous writing for further revision and to mail or deliver Super Revision 6 to an out-of-school audience. It is also possible at this point to expect students to collect and publish their best writings in personal booklets or to submit final drafts to contests or publishers.

LESSON THIRTY-EIGHT: FREEWRITING

Objective: The students will be able to

- Write freely about a friendship in Freewriting 13.

Procedure:

I. **PREWRITING:** Brainstorm about the meaning of *friend*.
    A. What is a friend? a true friend? a special friend?
    B. How does a friend behave?
    C. Do we have many "true friends" in a lifetime?
II. Read the following student paper about a friendship.

Roberta

We are only six, and it is summer all year long. Roberta and I dress in sailor dresses and wear our hair in French braids. Roberta has red hair and freckles, and she is beautiful.

We lick sour tasting medicine from our fingers, and sometimes Roberta forgets and sucks her thumb. Before supper we race to the corner to meet our fathers coming home on the bus from the Technicolor plant. When my father sees me he says, "Hi, ho!"

After supper, we take sides against Larry and Donny, and we tell them we hate them when they won't let us play. We count jacks in the shade of the avocado tree and act out Sleeping Beauty alongside the dusty, geranium hedge. Once, we kick Margo in the shin with my roller skate, and she tells her mother.

On my sister's birthday, we scrape all the lemon frosting off the cake before the party. When we hear the bell of the ice cream man, we race to beg nickels from our moms, and we buy pomegranates from the vegetable wagon man because the fruit inside looks like magic rubies, even if it tastes sour and makes our fingers red. We act out the story of Robin Hood and dress in long skirts and wear paper hats with feathers. Sometimes, we tie a rope to the roof of Larry's front porch, stand on the railing alongside the fuschia bushes, and swoop down on the sheriff's men.

One day I have the mumps and have to stay in bed. My cousin Jerry says, "You'll always look that way." I pull out the mirror I have hidden under my pillow to look at my fat face, and I cry. Roberta gives me half of her bubble gum, and I'm happy until she tells me, "I'm moving to Denver," and then I cry again.

On the day Roberta leaves, we stand side by side in our stocking feet on my front step, and we smile and pose while our mothers take pictures. I have hidden Roberta's shoes, and my mother is angry and says, "I don't care. Tell me where you put them. Right now!" So I tell, and then Roberta gets into the taxi, and I wave goodbye, and she waves back and then . . . I never ever see her again.

Naomi

III. The suggested topic for this freewriting is *friendship*. Encourage students to consider a friendship from their past rather than a current one. Teen-age friendships are often volatile or fleeting, while writing about a memory gives the student distance and perspective for the topic.

IV. Ask students to brainstorm on paper, answering the following questions:
   A. Write down as many names as possible of people you considered a "best friend" when you were young. Think of people of all ages.
   B. Alongside each name, write one or two word answers to the following:
      1. Where are these people now?
      2. Why did you like him or her?
      3. What did you do together?
      4. Think of a "once" that you shared with each.
      5. Did the friendships end? In what way?
      6. Is there any friend who is "lost"? (Someone with whom you've lost contact?)
   C. Now, zero in on one person—make a choice. As you begin to limit your topic, answer the following questions concerning the specific friend you have chosen.
      1. What were some of his or her physical characteristics?
      2. What was an expression he or she used often?
      3. Why were you friends?
      4. What did you share?
      5. What did you do for each other?
      6. What specific times were important to your friendship?
      7. Did the friendship end? Why?

V. Encourage students to brainstorm by clustering if this is a useful technique for them. Each person has his or her own unique writing process. Get students to choose the prewriting style most useful to them.

VI. **DRAFTING** Freewriting 13:
   Suggest that students visualize the friendship before they begin writing. Here is a sample instruction:

Put your pen or pencil down, close your eyes, and relax. Let your mind travel back to a memory of you and your friend. Feel yourself become smaller. You suddenly have to stand on tiptoe to reach something from a high shelf. You have to use two hands to open a door. Where are the two of you? What is the setting? What do you hear? Smell? What are you doing? What does your friend look like? What is the friend saying? What do you answer? Is this a happy or sad time? How can you tell? Watch this memory for as long as you'd like. When you are ready, begin freewriting about this friendship.

LESSON THIRTY-NINE: USING FLASHBACK

Objectives: The students will be able to

- Study the shape of a story.
- Practice using flashback.

Procedure:

    I. Ask the students to look over Freewriting 13 from the previous lesson.

        A. If their writing does not include direct dialogue, have them mark several places in the writing where it might be inserted.

        B. Give them time to write a brief scene or scenes in dialogue on separate paper. Explain they will be able to add the dialogue to their writing in their next draft.

    II. Good writing builds. It needs shape and direction. Hand out the accompanying worksheet, **Shaping: Going Somewhere**.

    III. Explain and discuss the handout with the students.

        A. Give students practice in shifting the chronology of a story by having them take part in a whole class activity.

            1. Explain they are to use *flashback* to rewrite the story of *Cinderella*.

            2. Suggest they may tell the story from either the Prince's or Cinderella's point of view. (Ask them to choose.)

            3. Place one of the following beginning lines on the blackboard:

                a. *Cinderella's foot slipped easily into the crystal shoe.*

                b. *The prince guided my foot into the glass slipper.*

            4. As you write their suggestions on the board, have all students contribute to a retelling of the story using a flashback.

        B. Next, ask each student to practice using flashback by doing the writing exercise at the end of the handout. After students have written for about ten minutes, you may wish to ask volunteers to read their beginning lines aloud.

    IV. Ask students to study the shape of their own Freewriting 13, and confer individually with them. What is the shape of the writing and what are the options for changing it? Is the writing told chronologically? Should it be kept that way? Could the student use a flashback, and would it improve the story? Perhaps a student is writing about how it used to be in comparison to how it is now. Is the student aware of this, and can he emphasize the contrast?

Name _____ Date _____

5.1 Shaping: Going Somewhere

Traditionally, students are expected to write outlines. Sometimes this is considered a first step in writing a paper. However, many professional writers seldom use outlines or use them only in the later stages of writing when they have gathered all the material they wish to use but want to order it in a particular way. You have been encouraged to freewrite your early drafts because freewriting allows your ideas to flow. You have been able to discover information, even surprises, as you've written.

As you've revised, you've learned to get rid of unnecessary words and repeated ideas *after* you've first written freely. However, a good piece of writing needs to go someplace. It needs to build toward a particular point. It needs a form or a shape, and yet there are no exact rules for shaping a writing. Unconsciously, you may have come to sense a form for your ideas. There are a few basic patterns you may have already discovered:

1. The *chronological story*—The writer begins at the beginning and tells what happens next and next until he or she gets to the end.

2. The chronological story is interrupted by a *flashback* to an earlier time. An author may use more than one flashback.

3. *Before and after*—The writer emphasizes how it used to be and how it is now. Contrast is an effective tool for writers.

Most freewritings are likely to be told chronologically. For you to practice telling a story with another shape, take a few minutes to write a story in a new way.

A Writing Exercise:

Write about the time you first successfully rode a bike or drove a car. Start at the moment of the success. Write from your own point of view or the point of view of a parent.

LESSON FORTY: BEGINNING AND ENDING

Objectives: The students will be able to
- Evaluate beginnings and endings.
- Revise the shape of their writing as Revision 5.

Procedure:

This lesson is likely to take *at least two class periods*.

DAY ONE

1. Distribute the accompanying handouts, **Beginnings and Endings** and **Student Sample**.

2. Read and discuss the handouts together. Explain the options the students have for beginnings and endings in their own Freewriting 13, and study the two drafts of Linda's paper.

3. Give the student writers time to work on their own papers, making adjustments and changes.

4. Confer with students about the first sentences or paragraph of each paper.

DAY TWO

1. Hand out and discuss the accompanying **Self-Evaluation Checklist for Shaping a Writing.**

2. Give students time for further revision.

3. Confer with students concerning the shape of their friendship writings as well as their beginnings and endings. (From this point, this writing is referred to as Revision 5.)

5.2 Beginnings and Endings

Writings that begin as freewritings need particular attention to both the beginning and ending. In a freewriting, it is natural to wander a bit before finding the real subject of a writing. Later, the excess needs to be cut. The same is true of endings, especially if the writing is chronological. It is difficult to know when to stop. The writer wants to give the reader enough information, but the danger is to give him too much. Try cutting out the last paragraph or two of a freewriting. It may help.

The opening (or *lead*) paragraph is critical to a writing because in these few lines the writer must catch the reader's attention. If opening lines are clever, or surprising, or imaginative, the reader will want to read on.

SOME OPTIONS FOR BEGINNING:

1. A few *short sentences*: "She was alone. It was dark. She was afraid."

2. *Set the scene*: "The kitchen was warmed by the morning sun. It was almost eighty degrees, and it wasn't even nine thirty. Outside the birds fluttered about, and a squirrel chirped on the wood pile."

3. *Foreshadowing* (a hint at what is to come): "I should have known better."

4. Just *begin the story*: "Somehow everyone melted into the background when he came into the room."

5. Try a *hook*: Begin with a word, action, or symbol and later come back to it. All that happens between the first and second telling makes the second appearance more significant than the first. Study both drafts in the **Student Sample.** You'll notice Linda moves a scream to the beginning of her second draft and mentions it again later. The scream hooks a reader and keeps her reading.

5.3 Student Sample

DRAFT 1

The way some people act toward old people makes me mad. I worked in a nursing home when I was fifteen. I worked on the ECF ward where the most senile people were. They were in highchairs and I can remember thinking how when you're young and can't sit up you're in a highchair and then here you are some 80–90 years older after having walked a lifetime of miles and you're back in a highchair. No progress at all.

All the older people were special in some way. One time I heard a scream from the men's ECF ward and dashed to where I heard the noise. It came from Bill's room. I frantically pulled at the closed door. It creaked open and there sat Bill in his wheelchair, a toothless grin on his face "Bill, what's wrong?" I asked him. "Nothing, Linnie, I was just practicin' in case of an emergency. Would you like to hear my woodpecker call?" "Bill, you scared me!" I said. He just smiled. A head nurse popped in the doorway. "Did a scream come from here?" she barked in her authoritative tone. Bill piped up, "That was me, this here girl was trying to hustle me and I was so happy I screamed." I looked at Bill and caught the wink the head nurse missed. She glared at Bill in disgust. "Bill, your are to be more quiet. Linda, You are never to come into this room again." Slam! The door shut. Bill looked at me sadly. I hugged him and said, "We'll see each other. She's not running a prison. Bill looked up at me with his usually happy eyes filled with tears and sadness. "Yes, she is. That's what this place is." I hugged him once more and left the room. We moved shortly after that incident. I was told Bill died. I cried for the old man who was my friend.

DRAFT 2: A LIFETIME OF MILES

"Ahhhhhh!" The scream came from the fifth room on the right side of the ECF ward and I rushed to answer it. I was working after school in a nursing home on the floor where the most senile patients were kept. They were strapped in high chairs or wheelchairs, and I remember thinking that when you're young and can't sit up, you're placed in a high chair and when you're old, some 80–90 years later after having walked a lifetime, you're back again in a highchair. No progress at all.

I heard the scream again. It came from Bill's room. I yanked at the closed door. "Bill, what's wrong?"

He smiled at me, "Nothing, Linnie, I was just practicin' in case of an emergency. Would you like to hear my woodpecker call?"

"Bill, you scared me," I sighed. He just smiled.

A nurse's head popped in the door. "Did a scream come from here?" she demanded.

Bill piped up, "That was me. This here girl was trying to hustle me, and I was happy so I screamed." He winked at me.

The nurse glared in disgust. "Bill, you are to be quiet. Linda, you are to get out and stay out of this room." Slam!

Bill looked at me sadly. Inside, I was crying for myself and for this old man who was my friend. I hugged him and said, "Don't worry, she's not running a prison. We'll see each other."

Bill shook his head and looked at me through tears. "Yes, she is. That's all this place is." And he turned his head away.

Linda

Name _____ Date _____

5.4 Self-Evaluation Checklist for Shaping a Writing

1. What shape does my writing have?

   Am I telling the story chronologically? _____

   Am I using a flashback, or should I use one? _____

   Am I contrasting the way it used to be and how it is now? _____

   Other? (Explain.) _____

2. Does the beginning make the reader want to read on?

   Have I used deliberately short sentences? _____

   Have I begun by setting the scene? _____

   Have I used foreshadowing? _____

   Have I used a hook? (What is it?) _____

   _____

3. Is the ending satisfactory?

   Does the story build? _____

   Does the story end at just the right place, or have I given the reader too much

   information? _____

   _____

LESSON FORTY-ONE: REVISING

Objective: The students will be able to

• Work on Revision 5 using a checklist.

Procedure:

This lesson may take *several class periods*.

    I. Distribute the **Self-Evaluation Checklist for Revision 5**.

    II. Review the checklist and ask students to revise and polish their writings as completely as possible to present to their peers in the small circle. (Indicate the date they are to be ready for peer evaluation.)

    III. Ask the students to work independently on their revisions as you confer with individual students.

Name _____ Date _____

5.5 Self-Evaluation Checklist for Revision 5

1. What is my purpose for this writing? _____

   _____

2. How am I telling this story? Chronologically? _____

   Flashback? _____

   Before and after? _____

   Other? _____

3. Do I have a strong beginning? _____

4. Am I satisfied with the ending? _____

5. What mood do I want to create? _____

6. Do I show the reader enough? _____

7. Have I used direct dialogue? _____

8. Have I included plenty of facts and specific details? _____

9. Have I avoided clichés? _____

10. Have I substituted strong verbs for weak ones? _____

11. Have I gotten rid of unnecessary words? _____

LESSON FORTY-TWO: REVISING AND PRESENTING

Objective: The students will be able to

• Complete Revision 5 and carry it through the entire writing process.

Procedure:

If you wish to have the students carry Revision 5 through the entire writing process, this lesson will take *six to seven class periods*.

Day One:	Students are assigned to new groupings for small group revision and are asked to respond to one another's writings using the same format as that used in Lesson Twenty-one. (If students are expected to make written as well as oral responses, more copies of the response sheet must be duplicated.)
Day Two:	Students continue to work on Revision 5, taking into account the comments and suggestions made by their peers in the small circle on the previous day.
Days Three and Four:	Students complete their revisions and work in pairs or with their teacher to edit for mechanical correctness.
Day Five:	Students complete a final, polished draft.
Days Six and Seven:	Students read their final drafts aloud in the large circle. Final copies are saved for Lesson Forty-three and for publishing in personal booklets. Grading, if necessary, happens at this point.

LESSON FORTY-THREE: SELF-ANALYSIS AND STUDENT TEACHER CONFERENCES

Objectives: The students will be able to

- Evaluate Revisions 1–5.
- Confer individually with the teacher about their progress as writers.

Procedure:

This lesson will take *several class periods,* depending upon how much time you wish to devote to student conferences. (Students may have previously evaluated Revisions 1–3 at the end of Lesson Thirty-three.) This lesson calls for a comprehensive evaluation of Revisions 1–5 and leads to a second, Super Revision of one of the writings in Lesson Forty-four.

I. Hand out the accompanying sheet, Analysis of My Writing.

II. Ask students to take their five revisions from their portfolios, or, if you have kept these revisions, return them to each student.

III. Ask students to study each writing and evaluate it.

IV. If possible, confer individually with each student using the student's self-analysis as a guide.

Name _____ Date _____

5.6 Analysis of My Writing

Analyze your writings:

Revision 1   Strengths: _____

_____

Weaknesses: _____

_____

Revision 2   Strengths: _____

_____

Weaknesses: _____

_____

Revision 3   Strengths: _____

_____

Weaknesses: _____

_____

Revision 4   Strengths: _____

_____

Weaknesses: _____

_____

Revision 5   Strengths: _____

_____

Weaknesses: _____

_____

Which writing improved the most from first to final draft? _____

What changes did you make? _____

If you were to deliver one of your writings to someone outside of school, which

writing would you choose? _____ Why? _____

_____ To whom might you send it? _____

LESSON FORTY-FOUR: PRESENTING A WRITING TO AN OUT-OF-SCHOOL AUDIENCE

Objective: The students will be able to

- Thoroughly polish a writing for an out-of-school audience as Super Revision 6.

Procedure:

This lesson will take *several class periods*.

I. Ask students to choose one writing from Revisions 1–5 to polish further in Super Revision 6 that will be delivered to an out-of-school audience.

II. Have the students designate a particular person to whom they will send the writing as a surprise gift. For example, they may choose a
   A. Parent.
   B. Grandparent.
   C. Relative.
   D. Someone mentioned favorably in the writing.
   E. Preferably an adult. (Up to this point, the students' audience has been limited to their teacher and peers; an adult audience outside of school offers new editing concerns and can also be highly encouraging to the student writer—see note from the student's journal on the following page.)

III. If possible, have your school furnish
   A. Envelopes.
   B. Postage.
   C. Cover letter (see accompanying sample). You may prefer to have students write their own cover letters.

      A less efficient and less expensive option is to have the students supply an envelope and postage. Students, however, like the idea of using an envelope with the school's return address. For some, this may be one of the few times the school sends good news.

IV. Have the students further revise and polish their papers using the accompanying **Self-Evaluation Checklist for the Super Revision**. Mechanical correctness *is* a concern in this revision. Encourage students to edit and confer with their peers and with you until a well-polished revision is produced. (Grading may happen here, if necessary.)

V. When students have completely polished their drafts, ask them to address the envelopes and enclose their writing and cover letter. (Review the correct way to address an envelope and to fold the pages to be included in the mailing.)

VI. Mail the letters.

A WORD OF ENCOURAGEMENT: The temptation may be to omit mailing the students' writing. The following are samples of responses students and teachers have received. Positive responses like these are sure to keep a teacher repeating this assignment.

Notes to the teacher:

"You and Tara did 'brighten' our day with Tara's memory writing—and your thoughtfulness."

"It was indeed a pleasant surprise on the day before Christmas to receive Amy's essay. Let me extend my sincere thanks to you for being so caring. . . ."

"How very thoughtful of you to share your student's work with us. The memory write-up of my granddaughter was very touching to me . . . . It brought the tears and happiness of fond memories."

From a student's journal:

"Remember the writings we had to send that you mailed with the stamp and envelope? I'd like to give you some of the credit, so 'thanks.' Craig, the guy I sent it to, called me up and said after he read it, it reminded him of the old memories we had. A couple of nights before I talked to him, I tried to call him, and his mom answered the phone. I said, "Hi, how ya doing, and she replied, "Oh, just fine." And then I knew it was coming. She said, "Matthew, we got your paper and read it. It was so nice. After I was through reading it, I cried and cried. It was just beautiful to receive." That made me feel real good. It was good talking to her and to have a nice feeling inside. So thanks again."

VII. There are three ideal places in this set of lesson designs for students to publish their best writings in their own personal booklets.
   A. If you intend to have students complete all the lessons suggested in this book, wait until Lesson Seventy-five to ask them to gather all their best writing into their own personal booklets.
   B. If you do not plan to have students complete all the writings suggested here, *this is a logical point* to arrange to have students publish their five revisions (and any extra writings) in personal booklets. Directions and suggestions for producing and publishing such booklets are included in Lesson Seventy-five.
   C. Another good point at which to have students gather and publish their writings occurs at the end of the poetry unit, Lesson Sixty-seven.

Throughout the year, encourage students to send writings to the school newspaper or magazine, local newspapers, and nationally circulated magazines that publish students' writing. The *Market Guide for Young Writers* by Kathy Henderson, published by Shoe Tree Press, Box 356, Belvidere, NJ, is updated annually and provides a complete description of a wide variety of publications which accept manuscripts from writers age 18 and under. Local newspapers frequently publish guest columns, and many offer student pages or may be willing to. Also keep students informed about writing contests.

Sample Cover Letter

(School's Letterhead)

November 1, 19 __

Dear _____ ,

    This envelope contains a surprise for you. _____
(Student's name)
and I hope it will be a day brightener.

    In our English class we have learned it is important for a writer to write for a particular audience, and the most recent assignment was for the student to choose someone special to send his/her writing.

    I am happy you were chosen as the *special* person. We all hope you enjoy the writing. Please remember to praise the author!

        Sincerely,

        Ms. Jones (teacher)

Name _____ Date _____

5.7 Self-Evaluation Checklist for the Super Revision

Read your paper over as if someone else has written it. Be tough with yourself. Check off each item after you have completed it.

_____ 1. Mark places where you are bored.

_____ 2. Mark places where you are confused.

_____ 3. Add
    A. MORE SPECIFIC WORDS:
       Instead of tree, *birch*.
       Instead of bird, *eagle*.
       Instead of dessert, *apple pie*.
    B. STRONG VERBS:
       Instead of ran, *darted or bolted*.
    C. DIRECT DIALOGUE: people speaking

    4. Cut
_____ A. UNNECESSARY OR OVERUSED WORDS: then, so, next.
_____ B. ADJECTIVES AND ADVERBS: if you've got two, consider cutting to one.
_____ C. CLICHES.

    5. Examine the shape of your writing.
_____ A. Does it have a good beginning?
_____ B. Is the ending satisfactory?
_____ C. Is the paragraphing appropriate?

    6. Proofread for mechanical concerns. An audience away from school *will* be concerned about correctness.
_____ A. Does each sentence begin with a capital letter?
_____ B. Does each sentence end with appropriate punctuation?
_____ C. Is each word spelled correctly?
_____ D. Are commas used correctly?
_____ E. Is the final copy neat and legible?

unit 6

APPEALING TO THE SENSES

Lessons Forty-five through Forty-nine encourage students to add sensory detail to their writing. Students do a freewriting in each lesson. You may have the students choose one of the five writings to carry through the entire writing process as Revision 7. However, in addition to practice with using all the senses, these lessons, along with Unit Seven, are intended primarily as a preparation for writing poetry in Unit Eight.

LESSON FORTY-FIVE: THE SENSE OF SIGHT*

Objectives: The students will be able to

- Understand the necessity for careful observation on the part of the writer.
- Practice emphasizing the sense of sight in Freewriting 14.

Procedure:

I. **PREWRITING**: Good writers are good observers. They remember sights, sounds, tastes, smells, and textures around them. It is likely that so far most student writing has relied primarily on the sense of sight. In the following days, students will practice using other senses as well. However, beginning with the sense of sight in this lesson helps convince each student of the need to become an even better observer.

    A. Ask the following observation questions, and have the students write their answers.
      1. What color are your math teacher's eyes?
      2. What color clothing was your mother or father or guardian wearing this morning when you left home?
      3. What color are the walls in your 6th period classroom?
      4. Can you describe precisely the colors of the walls in this classroom?

    B. Students probably have not been able to answer these questions with certainty. Emphasize the need for constant practice in observing accurately.

    C. Hand out the accompanying worksheet, **The Sense of Sight**. This is a simple exercise intended to focus thinking prior to Freewriting 14.
      1. Complete orally the exercises, emphasizing exact words and discussing the choices.
      2. Ask students to add sight words of their own in each category.

Some possible answers are the following:

Red	*Blue*	*Yellow*	*White*	*Black*
burgundy	royal	gold	cream	tar
cinnamon	teal	butterscotch	chalk	licorice
brick	midnight	fluorescent	enamel	pitch
flame	sapphire	chartreuse	platinum	

---

* Adapted from *Building English Skills*, Orange Level, (Evanston, IL: McDougal, Littell & Company, 1977), pp. 27–53; used by permission.

Purple	*Gray*	*Brown*	*Green*
orchid	ashen	almond	celery
grape	pearl	tan	avocado
violet	dove	cocoa	emerald
fuchsia	slate	walnut	

Appearance	*Movement*	*Shapes*
branching	Fast:	tubular
cracked	scramble	circular
ragged	gamble	conical
frayed	dash	shrunken
singed	scurry	sharp
rugged	Slow:	rectangular
sleazy	lumber	acute
tufted	slouch	crooked
hollow	stray	tapering
pasty	shuffle	clustered

D. Write the following words on the board: *a shoe, a leaf, bread, the sidewalk*.

E. Explain that each is something they might see every day. Ask students to choose one object, close their eyes and visualize a specific picture in their minds, and, finally, write several sentences, using the sense of sight, to create a picture which will be seen by the reader. For example, *A piece of soap* becomes "*a gold bar of DIAL, oval and cracked. The letters look like an old tombstone inscription. It has fallen from the sink and rests in the cobwebs and sand behind the waste basket.*

F. Encourage students to use original detail. For example, the description of the bar of soap is so particular that it could have existed only in that exact moment in that very place.

    1. Use the actual name of such things as streets (Bemidji Avenue, Birchmont Drive), cities (Nary, Duluth), and people (Aunt Ethel, Ron's son, Mark). Don't say: "*My only playmates were boys in the neighborhood.*" Say: *I was the only girl on Willobee Avenue, and in the summer I played "Ditch" with Donny Peterson, Larry Long, and Loren Nester.*

    2. Brand names are useful: Wheaties, Fruit Loops, 7-Up.

G. Ask students to read their sentences aloud, and have class members respond by pointing out exact detail in each writing which helps them to "see."

II. **DRAFTING** Freewriting 14: A sample direction.

A. For the remainder of the class period, write a description of a puddle of water.

B. Pick a particular season of the year and/or a particular location for your puddle. Is your puddle on a sidewalk or a road? What is the time of year? Perhaps your puddle is on the floor of a garage, or is it on a linoleum floor in a bathroom?

C. Make a list of specific details you might see when you observe this puddle.

D. Finally, freewrite a description of this puddle. Include as many specific facts as possible. Make your reader *see* your puddle.

6.1 The Sense of Sight

Sight words describe appearance, shapes, movements, and colors. In each sentence below, choose the word that creates the most specific picture for the reader:

1. Two squirrels (jumped, leaped) from branch to branch.

2. The thief was seen (loitering, walking) in the alley.

3. The colt's glossy coat gleamed (amber, brown) in the sun.

4. We all (ran, scrambled) to be first at the bus stop.

5. Sara's (freckled, spotted) face grew ashen in fear.

6. The (chubby, portly) two-year-old clapped his hands with delight.

7. The exhausted woman (plodded, walked) into the classroom.

8. The (dotted, dappled) fawn trailed after its mother.

SIGHT WORDS: Colors

Add additional words to each category:

Red	*Blue*	*Yellow*	*White*	*Black*
raspberry	aqua	straw	snowy	jet
cherry	navy	citron	ivory	ebony
tomato	steel	canary	pearl	_____
ruby	turquoise	butter	silver	_____
maroon	violet	lemon	milky	
_____	_____	_____	_____	
_____	_____	_____	_____	
_____	_____	_____	_____	
_____	_____	_____	_____	

Purple	*Gray*	*Brown*	*Green*
lavender	steel	sandy	mint
lilac	battleship	copper	lime
magenta	_____	rust	kelly
mauve	_____	bronze	olive
plum	_____	chocolate	_____
_____		_____	_____
_____		_____	_____

6.1 (cont'd)

Appearance	*Movement*	*Shapes*
dotted	fast	flat
blotched	hurry	round
wrinkled	skip	domed
patterned	sprint	curved
mottled	trot	wavy
shiny	bolt	scalloped
glossy	_____	ruffled
bright	_____	frilled
shimmering	_____	flared
glassy	_____	oval
flashy	_____	rotund
sheer	_____	chubby
opaque	_____	swollen
muddy	_____	lumpy
cheap	slow	padded
drab	creep	irregular
dingy	plod	angular
dull	tip toe	_____
old	amble	_____
used	slink	_____
worn	edge	_____
shabby	sneak	_____
chintzy	_____	_____
_____	_____	_____
_____	_____	_____
_____	_____	_____
_____	_____	_____
_____	_____	_____
_____	_____	_____
_____	_____	_____
_____	_____	_____
_____	_____	_____
_____	_____	_____
_____	_____	_____
_____	_____	_____

KEEP THESE SHEETS. CONTINUE TO ADD WORDS TO EACH CATEGORY, AND USE THEM AS YOU REWRITE AND REVISE YOUR PAPERS.

LESSON FORTY-SIX: THE SENSE OF HEARING*

Objectives: The students will be able to

- Practice appealing to the sense of hearing.
- Use the sense of hearing in Freewriting 15.

Procedure:

I. **PREWRITING:** Using the sense of HEARING.
   A. Ask students to write their answers to the following questions:
      1. Close your eyes and listen carefully. List all the sounds in this classroom you are able to hear.
      2. List ten sounds you like to hear. Use original detail. For example, instead of saying "the sound of a piano," say "the sound of my mother playing Debussy's *Girl with the Flaxen Hair.*
      3. List ten sounds you dislike. Use original detail. For example, "the cat gagging on a fur ball in the middle of the night."
   B. Have students share and discuss their answers.
   C. Hand out the accompanying exercise, **The Sense of Hearing.**
      1. Do the exercise orally.
      2. Ask students to add hearing words of their own to each category.
      3. Emphasize "noisy" words. The concept of *onomatopoeia*, words which imitate sounds, may also be introduced.

   Some possible answers:

Loud	*Soft*	*Speech*
bump	murmur	giggle
boom	twitter	scream
explode	patter	bellow
bray	hum	growl
stomp	swish	

   D. Write the following on the board: *a pep rally, an airport waiting room, the school cafeteria, an amusement park.*
   E. Ask students to pick one idea and spend some time listing the sounds they would hear at that location.
   F. When students have completed their lists, ask them to write several sentences or a paragraph describing the event using the sense of sound.
   G. When students have finished writing, ask each to read his or her sentences aloud.

---

* Adapted from *Building English Skills,* Orange Level (Evanston, IL: McDougal, Littell & Company, 1977), pp. 27–53; used by permission.

179

II. **DRAFTING** Freewriting 15: A sample direction.

For the remainder of the class period, freewrite a description with an emphasis on the way something sounds. Choose from the suggested list on the blackboard or pick a topic of your own. Brainstorm a list of sounds before you begin your draft. Imagine as much as possible for your reader.

Suggestions for the blackboard:

> *Waking up on a (spring, summer, winter, weekday, or Saturday) morning.*

> *Going to sleep late at night in the (spring, summer, or winter).*

Name _____ Date _____

6.2 The Sense of Hearing

Choose the word that creates the most vivid sound for the reader to hear.

1. A winter wind (crashed, whistled) through the birch trees.

2. Sam (bellows, sounds) like a bull when he is angry.

3. We heard the hens (peep, cackle) in alarm.

4. Our gang toasted wieners as the fire (crackled, burned) merrily.

5. The squeaking chalk (grated, scraped) on my ears.

6. Jane's (whining, piercing) voice rose above the crowd.

7. Jim (jingled, clanged) the coins in his pocket.

8. Sam gave a healthy (guffaw, giggle) when I told him the joke.

9. Raindrops (thumped, pattered) on the cottage roof.

HEARING WORDS

Add more words to each category:

Loud	*Soft*	*Speech*
crash	sigh	drawl
thud	whisper	whimper
thump	rustle	murmur
thunder	snap	chatter
smash	hiss	screech
screech	buzz	stammer
whistle	zing	stutter
squawk	tinkle	_____
rumble	clink	_____
grate	hush	_____
jangle	_____	_____
rasp	_____	_____
_____	_____	_____
_____	_____	_____
_____	_____	_____
_____	_____	_____
_____	_____	_____

LESSON FORTY-SEVEN: THE SENSE OF TOUCH*

Objectives: The students will be able to

- Practice appealing to the sense of touch.
- Use the sense of touch in Freewriting 16.

Procedure:

I. **PREWRITING:** Using the sense of TOUCH.
   A. Collect a variety of small objects.
   B. Ask for student volunteers.
   C. Blindfold the volunteers and ask them to identify by touch each of the objects you have collected.

   Another option: Place single objects in small paper bags, and pass the bags around the room. Ask members of the class to reach into each bag to identify the objects by touch.

   D. Hand out the accompanying exercise, **The Sense of Touch.**
      1. Do the exercise as a class.
      2. Ask students to add touch words of their own to each category.

   Some possible answers:

warm	hot	steamy
wet	leathery	silky
satiny	soft	smooth
furry	sandy	coarse

   E. Write the following on the board: *a piece of cotton, a blanket, noodles, a dry leaf, an ice cube, a warm bath, a sunburn.*
   F. Ask students to pick one idea and spend a few minutes thinking about how it feels. (Suggest a comparison.) Have them write several sentences that describe the feeling vividly. For example, *A toothache feels as if an ice cube is stuck to your tooth. It is a jabbing knife.*
   G. When students have finished writing, ask each to read his or her sentences aloud.

II. **DRAFTING** Freewriting 16: A sample direction.

---

* Adapted from *Building English Skills,* Orange Level (Evanston, IL: McDougal, Littell & Company, 1977), pp. 27–53; used by permission.

You have stretched your sense of touch, studied a list of touch words, and written several sentences. For the remainder of the class period, freewrite a description emphasizing the way something feels. Choose from the suggested list or pick a topic of your own. Brainstorm a list of ideas before you begin writing. Imagine for your reader as much as possible about how this journey would *feel*.

Suggestions for the blackboard:

1. *Walking along a beach or road on a hot day*
2. *Trudging through snow in January*
3. *Walking in the rain on a warm spring day*

Name _____ Date _____

6.3 The Sense of Touch

Choose the touch word that best creates a vivid picture.

1. Sam's frostbitten fingers felt (cold, numb).

2. The mud was (cold, mushy) under his feet.

3. Lisa felt (stabs, prickles) of fear as she entered the cave.

4. The (fuzzy, hairy) duckling ate from Sara's hand.

5. Jim refused to touch the (wet, slimy) seaweed.

6. A (bad, stabbing) pain shot through Joe's finger.

7. The old man's face was (tough, leathery) from the sun.

8. My aunt's (hairy, furry) coat keeps her warm.

TOUCH WORDS

Add additional words:

cool	_____	_____
scalding	_____	_____
sticky	_____	_____
damp	_____	_____
slippery	_____	_____
waxy	_____	_____
rubbery	_____	_____
crisp	_____	_____
velvety	_____	_____
woolly	_____	_____
feathery	_____	_____
fuzzy	_____	_____
hairy	_____	_____
gritty	_____	_____
sharp	_____	_____
thick	_____	_____

LESSON FORTY-EIGHT: THE SENSES OF TASTE AND SMELL*

Objectives: The students will be able to

- Practice appealing to the senses of taste and smell.
- Use the sense of smell in Freewriting 17.

Procedure:

I. **PREWRITING:** Using the senses of TASTE AND SMELL.
   A. Ask students to write answers to the following questions.
      1. What tastes do you like?
      2. What tastes do you dislike?
      3. What is your favorite food? Write a phrase describing that taste.
      4. What food do you most dislike? Write a phrase describing that taste.
      5. What are your favorite smells?
      6. What does your room smell like?
      7. What are some different kinds of stores? Describe how they smell.
      8. What are some classrooms in the school that have distinct smells?
      9. Can you think of a memory associated with a smell?
   B. Have students share and discuss their answers.
   C. Hand out the accompanying exercise, **The Senses of Touch and Taste.**
      1. Do the exercise together.
      2. Ask students to add words of their own to each category.

      Some possible answers:

Taste	*Smell*
buttery	perfumed
fruity	earthy
medicinal	briny
stale	sulphurous

   D. Write the following on the board: *a lemon drop, a piece of toast, a blade of grass, a pencil, a fire, toothpaste.*
   E. Ask students to pick one idea, to spend a few minutes "tasting" or "smelling" the object, and then to write a sentence that describes it vividly. For example, *The wet coat smelled of mothballs.*

---

* Adapted from *Building English Skills,* Orange Level (Evanston, IL: McDougal, Littell & Company, 1977), pp. 27–53; used by permission.

185

      F. When students have finished writing, ask each to read his or her
          sentence aloud.

II. **DRAFTING** Freewriting 17: A sample direction.

We are told that of all the senses, our memory for smells is the best. For
the remainder of the class period, write freely about one of your memories
associated with a smell.

6.4 The Senses of Taste and Smell

Choose the word that creates the most vivid picture.

1. An (acrid, horrible) smell remained long after the fire.

2. The rotting fish had a (putrid, unbearable) odor.

3. The air smells (wonderful, clean) after a summer thunderstorm.

4. Old coats can smell (bad, musty).

Add additional words to each category:

TASTE WORDS	SMELL WORDS
oily	sweet
salty	fragrant
bitter	minty
sweet	spicy
sugary	fishy
bland	acidy
sour	burnt
spicy	putrid
peppery	sour
burnt	rancid
raw	moldy

LESSON FORTY-NINE: USING ALL THE SENSES*

Objectives: The students will be able to

- Practice writing from another point of view (personification).
- Practice using all five senses in Freewriting 18 and choose one writing for Revision 7.

Procedure:

This lesson may take *up to eight class periods,* if you choose to have the students take one of their freewritings through the entire writing process. If not, save the freewritings. They will be used as prewritings for poetry in Unit Eight.

I. **PREWRITING:**

Read from *The Metamorphosis* by Franz Kafka, a story about a man who wakes up one morning to find he has turned into a giant insect, or read the following student sample:

THE TYPEWRITER

I sit on my table in Mrs. Smith's classroom smelling the geraniums and dust and waiting for someone to come. I'm hungry for a good meal of zesty electricity, but no one feeds me. I'm helpless until someone attaches my tail to an outlet, and then electricity courses through my body, and my heart hums with happiness. Suddenly, a boy with gritty hands bumps me. He sticks sweaty paper into my mouth and twists my ear. His calloused fingers press my keys, and I flick my letters against the paper in protest. My mind works wildly, and I invent wonderful stories, but just to get even, I deliberately mis-spell somee words. My head jerks to the left, and a bell clangs in my ear. Sometimes the boy misses my keys, and then he rubs the paper angrily with an eraser. Rubber bits tickle my ribs. When he's finished, he pulls the paper out of my grasp and knees me in the stomach. He forgets to cover me, and I sit in the burning sun. Chalk dust itches my smooth black skin. I'm sad and lonely, and I stop humming.

Jeff

II. Ask students to imagine a similar situation. Suppose they've suddenly been turned into one of the objects in the classroom—a chair, a desk, a blackboard. Perhaps, they've become something in a refrigerator—a

---

* Adapted from *Building English Skills,* Orange Level (Evanston, IL: McDougal, Littell & Company, 1977), pp. 27–53; used by permission.

188

carton of milk, an orange, a head of lettuce. Ask students to brainstorm with you on the blackboard about objects they might become. Their list may be similar to the following:

a worm	a pillow	a car	a bird (pick a specific kind)
a snake	a bee	a stone	an animal (choose one)
a window	a fence	a rug	a telephone
a rug	a weed	a tooth	a hockey puck
a pencil	a tree	a deer	the deer hunter's gun

III. Have students brainstorm about the possibilities for life as this new object. If a student becomes an ant, for example, the ant would usually live in a dark world. What would it feel like? Sound like? Look like? He has to search for food. What tastes would he most enjoy? What dangers would he face? What would be his job in his society? Some additional questions he might consider are: As an ant, what would you think about? What are your hopes and dreams? What would you fear?

IV. **DRAFTING** Freewriting 18: Write freely about being this object. Appeal to *all the senses* in your writing.

V. When the freewriting is completed, have students revise and edit briefly, making an additional effort to appeal to each of the senses. Ask them to volunteer to read their drafts out loud.

Note: Freewritings 14–18 will be used again in Unit Eight. Remind students to save them in their folders.

An option: You may want the students to choose one of the freewritings in this unit to carry through the complete writing process as Revision 7. If so, the schedule may be as follows: Day One, students revise independently; Day Two, peer groups convene; Day Three, independent revision; Day Four, revision for mechanical correctness with work in pairs; Day Five, final draft; Days Six and Seven, large circle.

unit 7

PLAYING WITH WORDS

Writers play with words. Lessons Fifty through Fifty-three involve creative activities and exercises which allow students to do this. These lessons are intended to be a preparation for poetry in Unit Eight but may also be used independently.

LESSON FIFTY: CREATING IN GROUPS

Objectives: The students will be able to

- Practice working in groups.
- Practice problem solving.
- Practice analyzing group processes and creative thinking.

Procedure:

This lesson provides practice with group dynamics and creativity. Although the writing groups are likely to have been functioning well, this activity allows students to analyze group processes, approaches to problem solving, and the creative process. Although the exercise, itself, is not "literary," students enjoy this activity, and it offers a refreshing change of pace at this point in the workshop.

I. Assign students to groups of four.

II. Each group receives a package of 3" by 5" cards and a roll of masking tape or adhesive tape.

III. Give the following instructions:

You are to build a tower made from the cards and tape. It will be judged on the basis of originality of design, height, and stability. You will have twenty minutes (or however much class time you wish to designate) to plan and build your structure. You may spend as much of your time as you wish in planning, or you may begin to build immediately, but your total time will be limited to twenty minutes. I will advise you of the time every five minutes and also three minutes before the time is up.

IV. Although each group begins with the same materials, allow students to use additional classroom materials such as scissors or colored markers if the possibility occurs to them.

V. At the end of the allotted period, call time and allow students to move from structure to structure, observing each. Have the students select the best construction, or bring in a judge from outside the classroom.

VI. Finally, ask each group to write a short analysis of how the group worked together to plan and build the tower. Papers may be read aloud.

VII. Encourage students to discuss the creative process. Some of their conclusions may be

A. Creativity involves a sense of play. Creative people often have a good sense of humor and are able to see unusual connections. Play can be productive.

B. Creativity involves taking risks, seeing the world in a new way.

C. Creative activities involve "what if" questions.

D. Creativity involves positive brainstorming. The creative person is likely to see possibilities in an option rather than its negative points.

E. After the initial stage of experimentation, creativity also weeds out ideas that don't work. To be creative is to strive after quality as well as originality. (Students often mistakenly believe that creativity is a legitimate excuse for shoddy work. Nothing can be farther from the truth.)

LESSON FIFTY-ONE: ETYMOLOGIES

Objectives: The students will be able to

- Understand that words have both denotative and connotative meanings.
- Understand that words have interesting histories.

Procedure:

Students will need dictionaries for this exercise. Be sure the available dictionaries have usage labels and etymologies.

I. Writers play with words. They are interested in their histories, their definitions, and their emotional impact.
   A. As an introductory exercise, ask students to do a word chain.
   B. Have them place the word *some* at the top of their paper.
   C. Explain they are to change one letter at each step to create a new word, finally arriving at the word *lark*.

   a solution: *some, same, lame, lace, lack, lark.*

   D. Next, encourage students to see how many words they can generate with a word such as *pot, sit, like, mine,* or *save.*

II. Words are fun. Place the words *denotation* and *connotation* on the board and define each.
   A. Denotation—the association that a word or phrase usually elicits, a factual definition. (example: *house*)
   B. Connotation—a secondary meaning of a word or phrase involving an emotional response. (example: *home*)

III. Explain the format of the dictionaries to be used for this exercise. How are the definitions arranged, for example? How will students recognize labels and etymologies? Where will they find an explanation of the abbreviations used in the entries?

IV. Hand out the worksheet, **All Kinds of Words.**
   A. Assign students to small groups.
   B. Ask them to complete the sheets, using their dictionaries if necessary.
   C. Discuss the students' answers when the work is completed.

   Some possible answers:

   1. man, wife
   2. radar, photocopy, toxic waste, user-friendly, yuppie
   3. leechcraft (medicine), bellytimbers (food)

193

4. o.k.
5. I, a, and, to, of
6. pneumonoultramicroscopicsilicovolcanoconiosis (lung conges-
tion)
7. a, I
8. kindergarten
9. spaghetti
10. lingerie
11. baseball, jazz
12. farm servant, scoundrel
13. innocent, foolish
14. ordinary person, one who is crude
15. foolish, agreeable
16. generally known, unfavorably known

V. Hand out the worksheet **Etymologies** and have the student groups use
    dictionaries to complete it. When students are done, take some time for
    discussion.

    Answers (These may vary from dictionary to dictionary. A
    small paperback dictionary is unlikely to include complete ety-
    mologies.): The *Oxford English Dictionary* is the best resource
    for etymologies.

    1. St. Mary's of Bethlehem (an insane asylum)
    2. alive
    3. cover the fire
    4. eye of the wind
    5. on the left hand
    6. crane's foot
    7. after Old Kinderhook club which supported Martin Van Buren
    8. river horse
    9. hairy cat
    10. wrings the nose or nose twist

Name _____ Date _____

7.1 All Kinds of Words

If necessary, use a dictionary to complete this exercise.

1. Think of some of the oldest words in the English language which are still commonly used today.

2. Think of some of the newest words in our language.

3. List some outdated words. (These will be labeled *archaic* in most dictionaries.)

4. Think of an English word which is recognized and used all over the world.

5. Think of some of the most frequently used words in our language.

6. List the longest word you can find and give its definition.

7. What are the shortest words in the English language?

8. Name a common English word borrowed from German.

9. Name a common English word borrowed from Italian.

10. Name a common English word borrowed from French.

11. Name words that originated in the United States.

The definition of some words has changed dramatically over time. *Angel* once meant *messenger,* and *governor* once meant *steersman.* Check the following words and explain how their meanings have changed.

12. Villain

13. Silly

14. Vulgar

15. Nice

16. Notorious

Name _____ Date _____

7.2 Etymologies

Many English words have interesting etymologies (word histories). The word *bonfire,* for example, was originally *bone fire* and was used in the Middle Ages when a plague swept Europe, killing over a third of the population. The bodies of the victims were burned to prevent further spread of the disease. Check the bracketed information in your dictionary and explain the original meaning of the following words.

1. bedlam _____

2. quick _____

3. curfew _____

4. window _____

5. sinister _____

6. pedigree _____

7. O.K. _____

8. hippopotamus _____

9. caterpillar _____

10. nasturtium _____

LESSON FIFTY-TWO: PLAYING WITH WORDS

Objectives: The students will be able to

- Recognize that writers often invent and play with words.
- Work with connotative meanings.

Procedure:

I. Read excerpts from books by authors such as Shel Silverstein or Dr. Seuss. Students will recall these books fondly. Point out that authors play with words.

II. Distribute the worksheet **Daring Definitions**.

III. Give students time to work on their own; then discuss their answers.

Some possible answers: 1. hungry cannibal; 2. crazy reason; 3. Russian boat carrying friends; 4. disease of astronauts; 5. moved rapidly; 6. burned or charred mail, dirty letter; 7. flowers; 8. head covering for children, juvenile delinquent; 9. bargain; 10. our male child.

IV. Distribute the worksheet **Reversals**. You may need to do the first question with them, as the instructions are complicated.

V. Give students time to work independently; then discuss the answers. Encourage them to work out a palindrome of their own.

answers: 1. raw, war; 2. live, evil; 3. star, rats; 4. reed, deer; 5. pan, nap; 6. devil, lived; 7. strap, parts; 8. sub, bus. Other palindromes: Madam, I'm Adam; Poor Dan is in a Droop.

VI. Hand out the worksheet **Playing with Words: Connotations**, and give students plenty of time for this sheet. Discuss this the next day, if necessary.

some possible answers: 1. cucumber; 2. swansong; 3. pits, dogmatic hullabaloo, doggerel, gumption; 4. swoosh (blue); 5. muffle, fluffy; 6. hiss, crunch, sizzle; 7. burp, belch; 9. lavender, chimes, dawn, golden, hush, lullaby, luminous, mist, tranquil, murmur; 10. cacophony, crunch, flatulent, gripe, jazz, phlegmatic, plutocrat, grunt, croak, pus.

197

Name _____ Date _____

7.3 Daring Definitions

Many English words, when analyzed logically, could have meanings quite different from their real ones. For example, the word *parapets,* which is a high, defensive wall, could mean *two dogs.* Invent a silly definition for each of the following words:

1. gladiator _____

2. locomotive _____

3. comradeship _____

4. mistletoe _____

5. ransom _____

6. blackmail _____

7. bloomers _____

8. childhood _____

9. good-bye _____

10. arson _____

Think of some words of your own, and invent your own daring definition:

Name _____ Date _____

7.4 Reversals

What do you get when you spell a word backward? Usually nothing that is understandable or even pronounceable. Some words in English, however, spell other words when reversed. In the left-hand column below are definitions of words which, when reversed, yield words whose definitions are in the right-hand column. Can you identify each pair?

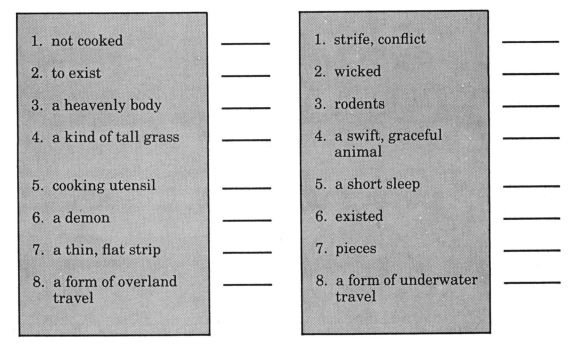

Left column		Right column	
1. not cooked	_____	1. strife, conflict	_____
2. to exist	_____	2. wicked	_____
3. a heavenly body	_____	3. rodents	_____
4. a kind of tall grass	_____	4. a swift, graceful animal	_____
5. cooking utensil	_____	5. a short sleep	_____
6. a demon	_____	6. existed	_____
7. a thin, flat strip	_____	7. pieces	_____
8. a form of overland travel	_____	8. a form of underwater travel	_____

According to some language experts, the most difficult kind of phrase to create is a *palindrome,* a sentence of group of sentences that reads the same backward and forward. Consider the following:

Red rum, sir, is murder
A man, a plan, a canal—Panama
Ma is as selfless as I am.
He lived as a devil, eh?
Nurse, I spy gypsies. Run!
Able was I ere I saw Elba.

Try creating a palindrome of your own:

Name _____ Date _____

7.5 Playing with Words: Connotations

How many words do you know? 20,000? 30,000? Not enough. A ten-year-old knows as many as 100,000. Still not enough. Never enough. You need all the words in the world to express your ideas. Writers are word watchers, word hoarders, word users. Get in the happy habit of playing with words.

1. What is your favorite word?

2. What word sounds sad without naming something sad?

3. What word makes you laugh?

4. Aside from the name of a color, what is the most colorful word you can think of?

5. What are some quiet words?

6. What are some noisy words?

7. What is an undignified word?

8. Make a list of the ten most beautiful sounding words you can think of:

   _____   _____

   _____   _____

   _____   _____

   _____   _____

   _____   _____

9. Make a list of the ten worst sounding words you can think of:

   _____   _____

   _____   _____

   _____   _____

   _____   _____

LESSON FIFTY-THREE: INVENTING LANGUAGE

Objective: The students will be able to

- Study invented language and invent words of their own.

Procedure:

    I. Writers often invent language. If possible, read from Lewis Carroll's *Jabberwocky*.

    II. Ask students to give examples of other invented literary language.
        A. *Clockwork Orange,* Burgess
        B. *Watership Down,* Adams
        C. *Lord of the Rings,* Tolkien

    III. Ask students whether they can think of any words their friends or families have invented and used. (Some students may know pig Latin. The first letter or sound of a word is dropped and moved to the end of a word and the letters *ay* are added. For example, *Ancay ouyay eakspay igpay atinlay?* is "Can you speak pig Latin?")

    IV. Hand out the accompanying sheet, **Inventing Language.**

    V. Work through the sheet with the students. Give them plenty of time to work independently on the section concerning Sniglets.

        answers:
        UNICEF—United Nations International Children's Emergency Relief Fund
        ROM—read-only memory
        RAM—random access memory
        radar—radio detecting and ranging
        laser—light amplification by stimulated emission of radiation
        ZIP code—Zone Improvement Program
        scuba—self-contained underwater breathing apparatus
        SASE—self-addressed, stamped envelope

motel (motorist + hotel)	splatter (splash + spatter)	flurry (flutter + hurry)
motorcade (motor + cavalcade)	squawk (squall + squeak)	
brunch (breakfast + lunch)	twirl (twist + whirl)	

7.6 Inventing Language

Acronyms are words derived from the first letters of words in a phrase.

CARE—Cooperative for American Remittances to Europe
AWOL—Absent without leave

Do you know what these acronyms stand for?

1. UNICEF _____
2. ROM _____
3. RAM _____
4. radar _____
5. laser _____
6. ZIP code _____
7. scuba _____
8. SASE _____

Invent your own acronyms by working backward from words like DOPE, SOLO, KIDS, FOOL, FUN, LOVE, SENIOR, GRADUATE. For example, SMILE is *Something Mandatory in Laughing Effectively.*

_____
_____
_____

Some words are blended. For example, smog is a blend of "smoke" and "fog." Can you figure out what words might have been blended for the following?

1. motel _____
2. motorcade _____
3. brunch _____
4. splatter _____
5. squawk _____
6. twirl _____
7. flurry _____

Where do you suppose these cities are located?

1. Calexico, California _____
2. Kanorado, Kansas _____

Invent some blended words of your own. For example,
BLUSHED + GIGGLED = _____
Can you think of others? _____
_____
_____

7.6 (cont'd)

Rich Hall and Friends in the book *Sniglets** make up names for objects or actions that have previously gone nameless. For example,

1. chwad: hard, little pieces of gum occasionally lodged under chairs or tables
2. flen: the black, crusty residue found on the necks of old ketchup bottles
3. lub: any large particle of food that becomes stuck between the teeth

Invent a *Sniglet* for each of the following:

1. The act of blowing a bit of breath into your nose to see if the garlic you've just eaten has given you bad breath. _____
2. The act of tucking one's shirt with one hand while a finger carefully checks to see if one is properly zipped up. _____
3. The act of opening one's eyes slightly to see if one's kissing partner has his or her eyes open. _____
4. Someone else's hair that always seems to clog the shower drain. _____
5. Belly button lint. _____
6. Pencil erasure remnants. _____
7. An expert at writing *Sniglets*. _____
8. Turning the bathtub faucet on and off with your toes. _____
9. The sticky goo left over after tape is removed. _____
10. The black ring around the base of a two-liter soda container. _____
11. Invent some of your own.

---

unit 8

WRITING POETRY

Lessons Fifty-four through Sixty-eight are a design for a three-week poetry unit. Students begin by reading published contemporary poetry in search of their own definition of poetry. The earliest lessons are based on simple poetic forms. More complex forms and concepts are introduced as the lessons continue. The unit provides directions for twelve poems and may culminate in publication of individual student booklets.

LESSON FIFTY-FOUR: READING AND DEFINING POETRY

Objectives: The students will be able to

- Find samples of poetry they like.
- Begin to make a definition of poetry which is useful for them in their own writing.
- Share a favorite poem with the class.
- Begin recognizing poetic elements.

Procedure:

This lesson requires *two class periods*.

For the next three weeks, students will write poetry. Although they may wish to work with rhyme, this unit does not require it. Suggested assignments call for free verse with specific structures and shapes. The lessons are useful in emphasizing the power of economy, contrast, repetition, and figures of speech in any writing whether it is poetry or prose. Don't encourage students to use rhyme until they have practiced other poetic skills. Rhyme sidetracks them from using other important elements and tempts them to say that which they don't intend.

DAY ONE

1. Bring a collection of contemporary poetry books from the library to class, or arrange for the class to read and work in the library. Give students at least one class period to read and look through as many books as possible.
   a. Ask students to read widely and find at least one poem they each honestly like. Don't let them rely on an old favorite, but expect them to read to discover something new.
   b. Explain they will be expected to share a poem with the class in the large circle on the following day. They should be prepared to explain in detail why they admire the poem they have chosen.

DAY TWO

1. Arrange the class in the large circle and ask the students to take turns reading and discussing the poems they have chosen. (Begin the session by sharing several poems you have found. Model an explanation of why they appeal to you.) Encourage the students to explain why they were attracted to their poems. Ask questions, if necessary, to elicit more thoughtful answers.
2. Most students are likely to choose a poem because the subject matter appeals to them. They are unlikely to be aware of any poetic devices the poet may be using. If so, this is a good time to reinforce the idea that the

subject matter of poetry is ordinary human experience. It is important for students to realize *their own experience is subject matter for poetry*. Occasionally, point out poetic elements in particular poems as you hear them read.

3. After the poems have been read and each student has discussed a poem, ask the whole class to brainstorm a list on the board of some elements of poetry. The list may be similar to the following:

subject matter—feelings (both serious and humorous)
economy (grammar and usage rules are sometimes ignored)
shape or pattern
white space
line breaks
repetition of words or phrases
rhythm
rhyme
voice of a speaker
verbs
images (pictures in the reader's head)
appeals to all the senses
word sounds (alliteration, onomatopoeia)
figures of speech (simile, metaphor, personification, onomatopoeia, hyperbole, oxymoron)
surprises!

LESSON FIFTY-FIVE: A LIST POEM

Objective: The students will be able to

- Write Poem 1 based on a list, emphasizing repetition and a new voice.

Procedure:

I. **PREWRITING:**

A. Remind students that as children, we heard many "don'ts."

B. Ask them to brainstorm a list of all the "don'ts" they remember from their childhoods. For example, "Don't talk back!" Ask the students to begin each line of their list with the word *don't*. Peter Elbow in *Writing with Power* (New York: Oxford University Press, pp. 102–116), suggests: "I Wish" or "Once" as also being helpful starters for poems such as this.

C. When students have finished brainstorming, ask them to place an asterisk alongside the most serious admonition.

II. **DRAFTING:**

A. Explain the structure of Poem 1.

1. The title is the student's name or the name a parent might have used for him or her when the parent was especially irritated.

2. Every subsequent line begins with the word "don't."

3. The last line, reserved for the most serious admonition, begins "And never, never, ..."

B. When the draft is completed, point out to the students that their poems say something true about each of their childhoods and is spoken in the *voice* of a parent.

III. **REVISING:** Give students a plain, white sheet of paper and ask them to use the entire page of paper for the poem, *shaping* it in any way they wish, and making good use of the *white space* in the design of their final copy.

IV. **PRESENTING:** Ask students to read their poems aloud. (If you plan to have the students publish all their poems in personal booklets, collect the polished copies and save them for the appropriate time.)

LESSON FIFTY-SIX: A CONCRETE POEM

Objectives: The students will be able to

- Understand "shaping" a poem.
- Write Poem 2, a concrete poem.

Procedure:

I. PREWRITING

A. As a warm-up, draw the following riddles on the board and ask students to solve them. The rebus, created from combinations of words, letters, syllables, figures, or symbols, is positioned to create disguised words or phrases, names, places, or sayings. (Encourage students to invent more of their own.)

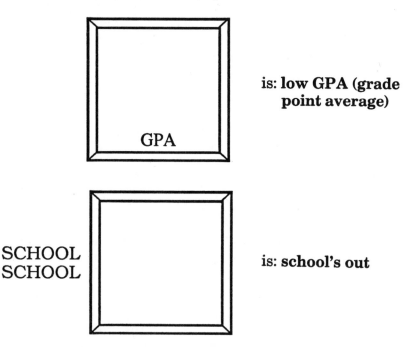

is: **low GPA (grade point average)**

is: **school's out**

B. Hand out the worksheet, **Solving a Rebus**. Give students time to try to discover the solutions.

Answers: 1. No running in the halls. 2. Final exam. 3. Big date on Friday. 4. Teacher's pet. 5. Reasonable teacher. 6. Late for class. 7. Flunk out. 8. Skip day. 9. He's an under achiever. 10. Graduate. 11. Sent down to the office. 12. Being among friends.

C. Point out samples of concrete poetry found in books in the library collection.

208

D. Distribute the accompanying **Samples of Concrete Poetry.**

E. Explain that concrete poems play with words and shapes. Some poems are shapes filled in with words; in other poems words may outline a shape or imitate a movement.

F. Read the following brainstorming questions aloud to the students:

1. Think of a funny thing a pet has done.
2. What makes you happy today?
3. What one thing would you like to teach someone?
4. Name a favorite sport. Why is it your favorite?

II. DRAFTING

A. Ask each student to follow these steps in writing a concrete poem (Poem 2).

1. Decide what you want to write about. It should be a visible thing, like a dog or skyscraper.
2. Decide what you want to say. Jot down words or phrases that come to mind.
3. Expand one idea into several phrases or sentences. Some concrete poems are complete sentences; others use single words.
4. Outline the shape of an object with words, or fill in the shape, or trace the movement of an object.

B. Concrete poetry doesn't have to rhyme or have a certain number of words or syllables.

C. Encourage students to try several concrete poems.

III. REVISING: Distribute plain white paper and have students write the final draft. Remind them to design their poems with the whole page and the white space in mind.

IV. PRESENTING: Encourage students to view one another's final drafts. Collect the final drafts of Poem 2. You may wish to display them around the room.

Name _____ Date _____

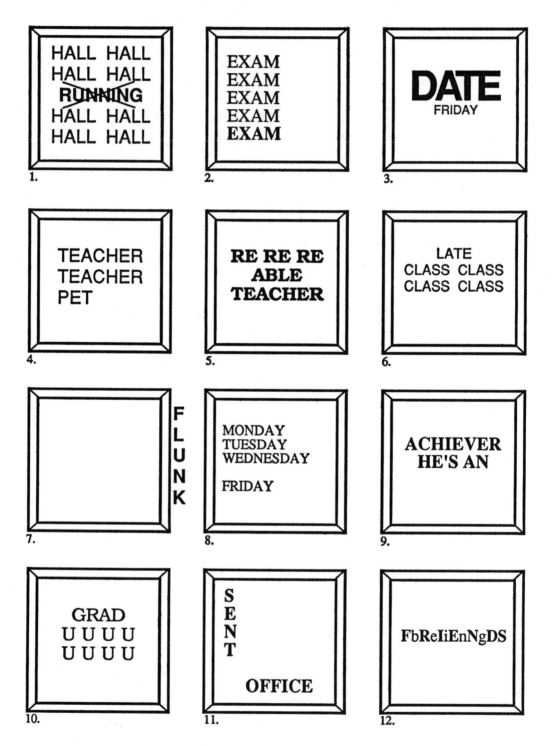

1.
HALL HALL
HALL HALL
R̶U̶N̶N̶I̶N̶G̶
HALL HALL
HALL HALL

2.
EXAM
EXAM
EXAM
EXAM
EXAM

3.
DATE
FRIDAY

4.
TEACHER
TEACHER
PET

5.
**RE RE RE
ABLE
TEACHER**

6.
LATE
CLASS CLASS
CLASS CLASS

7.
F
L
U
N
K

8.
MONDAY
TUESDAY
WEDNESDAY

FRIDAY

9.
**ACHIEVER
HE'S AN**

10.
GRAD
U U U U
U U U U

11.
S
E
N
T

OFFICE

12.
FbReIiEnNgDS

Name _____ Date _____

8.2 Samples of Concrete Poetry

a white butterfly flutters and tumbles then flips and twists but always dodges and dips and lands on a flower

A
raindrop
dives from a
cloud, patters
on a roof, splashes
into a puddle, bathes
a car, nourishes a
garden, slides down
a rain barrel, hangs
from a clothes line, perches
on a flower petal,
glistens like a
diamond, and
dies in the
sun.

My friends call it ugly and laugh, my parents call it unreasonable and ask why would I need a car in Holland, anyway Flat tires can always be fixed Grandma won't be driving much longer anyway This tire is quite old & slipshod Rust is easy to get off It's inexpensive dent. Antennaes can be bent straight But this car is old and neat and a Jeep

LESSON FIFTY-SEVEN: SHAPING POETRY FROM PROSE

Objective: The students will be able to

- Shape their own prose into Poem 3, making use of line breaks and white space.

Procedure:

I. PREWRITING:

A. Ask students to look over their earlier Freewritings 14–18 and select one to shape into a poem.

B. Hand out and discuss the accompanying sheet, **Form in a Free Verse Poem**. Study the samples of student prose and note the changes made as the prose becomes free verse.

C. Ask students to shape their own prose into poetry.

1. Direct students to underline interesting words or phrases in their original freewriting. They should underline anything that captures an idea or feeling, appeals to the senses, or creates images. Encourage them to underline good verbs and figures of speech. Quantity is important here. (Not every word or phrase chosen at this point will have to be used later.)

2. Next, ask students to rewrite the underlined words or phrases on a second page, experimenting with shaping and arranging the lines in a variety of ways to make use of line breaks and white space.

3. Another option: Place the following prose on the board.

> I see a man standing with a fish on his line. The man smiles. The fish is helpless, suspended by a piece of string. It reminds me of a yoyo going up and down with no control of its own. The man grins, frees the fish, lets it go. It was too small to keep.

D. Have the whole class offer suggestions for making changes and inserting line breaks.

E. The rough draft of a class poem may be similar to this:

> I see a man
> with a fish
> on his line.
>
> The fish,
> suspended
> on a piece of string
> like a yo yo,

glides up and down,
up and down.

The man grins,
frees the fish—
   too small
      to keep.

II. DRAFTING:

A. Encourage students to add, change, or improve word choices or phrases whenever they are aware of that possibility. (For example, change common verbs to colorful ones.) Try for unusual word arrangements and imaginative combinations.

B. More time will be given during the next lesson for additional revision and a final draft of Poem 3.

8.3 Form in a Free Verse Poem

1. A line is a unit of thought or feeling.
      It can be long. (a long or slow thought or feeling)
      It can be short. (a quick, choppy idea or feeling)
      A line can be one word if you want that word to stand out.

2. The position of a word in a line makes a difference.
      The reader notices the last word in a line, so if you break a line after a
         word, that word is stressed.
      The first word in a line is also in a strong position.
      If you want the reader to really notice a word, put it alone on a line.

3. A line can visually reflect what you are saying.

   The
         snowflakes
                    floated
                        down.

4. Line breaks can follow rhythms of speech. You can break a line instead of using
   punctuation.

      to put pauses where you want   them.

   (Some poems do not use punctuation. However, there must be some way to
   indicate pauses.)

5. Line breaks can give you subtle shifts in meaning from one line to the next.

      Pity the boy dreaming the hour away
      not.

6. Stanzas are like paragraphs in prose writing. Begin a new stanza with each
   new thought. In a poem with no punctuation, you may begin a new stanza each
   time you have the equivalent of a sentence.

7. White space is important in a poem. It is like the background or border of a
   picture. One poet has said that the white spaces are where the poem happens. It
   is space to separate ideas and let them sink in. The design a poem makes on the
   page is important. Lay out your poem on an entire page of paper with the entire
   sheet of paper in mind.

8.3 (cont'd)

SAMPLES OF PROSE SHAPED INTO FREE VERSE

Sample 1

Jumping on the merry-go-round, I scramble for a place to sit. There are kids scampering under my feet as the ride makes its first jerk ahead. The ride makes the dust come alive while slowly turning circles.

> Jumping on the merry-go-round,
> I scramble for a place to sit.
> Kids jostle and push
> As the ride jerks ahead.
> Dust dances delightedly and
> the ride turns round and round.
>
> Angie

Sample 2

During the summer I take long walks along the dirt road where we live. I usually walk when the sun begins to set in the sky. The sun casts long shadows on a road and brilliant colors in the clouds. A cool breeze blows through my hair bringing with it the smell of wild roses blooming in the ditches. The birds sing happily as they fly through the air and rest on a telephone wire. My dog, Rufus, runs ahead to chase animals into the bushes. I hear animals softly walking through the woods nearby. The roar of tractor engines can be heard in the fields and a cloud of dust rises from behind a tractor in the field. I go on walks to calm my nerves or to think about my problems. I feel the tension leave as I breathe in the fresh air and look at the world around me.

> The sun casts long shadows on a dirt road
> and colors the clouds.
>
> A breeze tip-toes through the trees
> teasing perfume from wild roses.
>
> A dog scolds animals into the woods and
> a cloud of dust swirls behind the tractor.
>
> A girl strolls slowly past the woods
> and returns home
>
> Anne

LESSON FIFTY-EIGHT: FIGURES OF SPEECH

Objectives: The students will be able to

- Understand alliteration, onomatopoeia, and oxymoron.
- Add some or all of these elements to their own poetry.
- Complete Poem 3.

Procedure:

This lesson may take *two class periods.*

I. In this lesson students will study alliteration, onomatopoeia, and oxymoron and will add these elements, if possible, to Poem 3.
   - A. Hand out the accompanying sheets, **Poetry and You** and **Figures of Speech**.
   - B. Read and discuss the worksheets. (Note: Other examples of oxymora are *awfully nice, bittersweet, completely unfinished, gentle torture, hot ice, happy loser, pleasant pain, happy tears, dry rain, fresh frozen, jumbo shrimp,* or *good grief.*)

II. **REVISING**
   - A. Ask students to revise their draft of Poem 3, adding alliteration, onomatopoeia, or oxymora when possible. Confer individually with students.
   - B. When students have completed their revisions of Poem 3, distribute unlined paper and encourage them to consider the whole page as they shape and design their final draft.

III. **PRESENTING:** If there is time, have students read the poems aloud to the class before turning them in. If there is little time remaining, collect the poems, and, before the next class period, read and pick out several good examples. At the beginning of the following class period, ask the authors of the poems you have chosen to read them aloud.

Name _____ Date _____

8.4 Poetry and You (the Poet)

A poem can be about anything, written in any form. There are no rules unless you make them yourself. Trust yourself and have fun.

A poem catches a part of your world in words. Poems play with words, images, sounds, rhythm, ideas. They make word pictures (images) so real, they can be seen with the mind's eye. They show rather than tell. They make the reader "see."

Poems make new connections between ideas and things, perhaps never put together before. Each poem is a new thing, and as the poet you have enormous power. Poems help us to see in new ways. They help us to tell the truth or to make up wonderful lies.

Unity of tone—Decide on the mood of your poem and make sure all elements fit it. Don't put a humorous comparison or detail into a serious poem unless you have reason to do it.

Unity of imagery—All of the images in a poem should be harmonious. One machine image in a poem of nature images can be jarring. Many poets use one kind of image throughout a poem. (For example, the prairie compared to the sea: grass, waves, gulls, vastness of space, farms as islands or ships.) Unity gives a poem a feeling of being finished and complete.

Economy—A poem that is compact and concentrated has more energy. The meaning is not spread out over many words, diluted like Kool-Aid with too much water in it. After the first draft is completed, get rid of extra words. Write in fragments if you wish. Try getting double duty out of words. For example, "The old woman sat in her rocking chair rocking back and forth, and the chair creaked as it rocked," can be shortened and strengthened by paring it to "The old woman creaked in her rocker." Finally, don't say too much. Let the reader meet you halfway and supply part of the meaning.

Experiment—The poet is free to experiment. There are no rules for a poem except those the poet makes. Writing a poem is playing with words and ideas and feelings—and it's magical!

8.5 Figures of Speech

ALLITERATION

Alliteration is the repetition of the initial *sound* in two or more words. Often it's the repetition of the initial letter, but not always. ("Fancy fish" is alliterative, but "celestial candles" is not.) Alliteration is the most popular of the figures of speech. Complete the following phrases (most of which are now cliches.)

. . . in the wild and _____ west.

I'll do or _____ !

The new miracle drug will _____ or cure.

Don't get on your _____ horse with me.

Sticks and _____ may break my bones . . . .

You can have fun with alliteration.

Create a tongue-twister. (Remember "Peter Piper picked a peck . . ."?) Choose a letter: *p* or *s* or *t* or any other letter you like. Use a dictionary if necessary and make a list of words beginning with the letter you choose.

_____ _____ _____ _____ _____

_____ _____ _____ _____ _____

_____ _____ _____ _____ _____

Combine as many of your words as possible into a nonsense sentence, and presto, you have created a tongue-twister:

_____

_____

ONOMATOPOEIA is the official term for words that *sound* like what they mean. Some of the more obvious examples are *buzzed, crackled, wheezed, droned, whimpered, shrieked, crunched, thundered, babbled, roared, hummed,* or *popped.* From this list, complete the following sentences.

1. Beneath her feet, the crystal snow _____.

2. The mosquitoes _____ at my window screen.

3. The child _____ happily over her blocks and balls.

4. The sheep dog, its paw torn and bleeding, _____ at the door.

8.5 (cont'd)

Add three words to each of the following categories:

"Cool" words: klink   whine   _____ _____ _____

"Hot" words: sizzle singe   _____ _____ _____

"Quiet" words: hiss   tap   _____ _____ _____

"Shapeless" words: splat   plop   _____ _____ _____

An OXYMORON is the blending of two contradictory terms. *Oxy* means sharp and *moros* means stupid. It is a sharp-stupid saying. *To make haste slowly* is an example. Fill in the blanks with words that are contradictory.

1. Your mother looks at your room and says, "A _____ mess!"

2. The doctor finishes examining you and says, "You're fine. You can do anything.

   You are _____ healthy."

3. As Juliet said to Romeo, "Parting is such _____ sorrow."

Create or recall other examples of the oxymoron. Aim for three.

LESSON FIFTY-NINE: SIMILE

Objectives: The students will be able to

- Define and recognize simile.
- Write Poem 4 using simile.

Procedure:

  I. **PREWRITING:**

    A. Define *simile:* a figure of speech that compares two objects using *like, as,* or *than. (She is as red as a rose. I slept like a log.)* The objects being compared are not similar except in one respect. The girl and the rose are unlike except they share a blushing quality. The tired boy and the log are different except for their inertia.

    B. Explain to students that Poem 4 will be based primarily on similes.

    C. Brainstorm on the blackboard for a list of words naming emotions.

    D. Provide the following structure for Poem 4. The poem is a definition using all the senses and similes which the students make personal by using original detail which reflects their lives and experiences.

       emotion is color. (This line is a metaphor.)
       It sounds like . . .
       It tastes like . . .
       It smells like . . .
       emotion feels like . . .

    A sample: *Indifference* is water-stained gray.
              It sounds like hissing static on the radio.
              It tastes like overcooked noodles.
              It smells like a musty, closed attic room.
              Indifference feels like a lukewarm bath in rusty water.

  II. **DRAFTING:** Ask the students to pick a word of their own from those brainstormed on the blackboard and begin their own poem. (Encourage students to include onomatopoeia in the description of sound.)

 III. **REVISING:** Have the students edit and shape their poems (adding specific original detail where appropriate, and writing their final copy on plain paper). Work individually with students.

 IV. **PRESENTING:** When the final copies are completed on unlined paper, ask students to read their poems aloud before collecting them.

LESSON SIXTY: METAPHOR

Objectives: The students will be able to

- Define and recognize metaphors.
- Write Poem 5 structured as a metaphor.

Procedure:

I. PREWRITING:

A. Write a metaphor on the blackboard:
   A caterpillar is an upholstered worm. (anonymous)

B. Define *metaphor*. The metaphor is first cousin to the simile. Like the simile, it compares two objects but does not use *like* or *as* or *than*.

   SIMILE: *Her cheeks are like polished apples.*
   METAPHOR: *Her cheeks are polished apples.*

C. Place the following sentences on the blackboard and ask students to complete each metaphor:

   1. My legs were _____ as I raced for the tape. (rubber bands?)

   2. Faced with failure, I felt my heart become a (an) _____ . (jackhammer?)

   3. As the audience listened in shocked silence, my fingers became _____ , stumbling over the ivory. (ice cubes?)

   4. My feet were _____ as I set out to investigate the peculiar noises coming from the attic. (cement blocks?)

D. Ask students to write a metaphor for their own family. (Poem 5)
   1. Distribute **Sample Metaphor Poems** or read them to the students.
   2. Have students brainstorm for a list of *units* on the blackboard. For example, *groceries, dishes, silverware, drawers, clothes, tools, chairs, furniture, books, buildings, closets, shoes or boots, windows.*

221

II. **DRAFTING:** Ask students to pick a particular unit and write a metaphor for their own family which includes every family member as an element in the unit.

III. **REVISING AND PRESENTING:** Confer individually with students. When all students have completed the poem and have written a final draft on unlined paper, have them take turns or volunteer to read aloud before turning in a final copy.

"A Metaphor Poem"

1) Begin by reading the 2 sample poems which are metaphors for families. Notice the imagery and the unity in each.

2) Brainstorm your idea(s) for metaphors which could show your family. (Make sure to include all members.)

3) Possible items you could compare to your family are probably endless. DON'T write, "I couldn't think of anything"!

4) Write your poem ....

5) If possible, use a poetic device or two like: onomatopoeia or alliteration or vivid imagery, etc....

6) Submit at end of class.

7) Have fun   (")

* P.S. Remember to turn in your poetry journal today!

8.6 Sample Metaphor Poems

Metaphor for a Family

My family lives inside a medicine chest:
Dad is the super-size band aid, strong and powerful
    but not always effective in a crisis.
Mom is the middle-size tweezer,
    which picks and pokes and pinches.
David is the single small aspirin on the third shelf,
    sometimes ignored.
Muffin, the sheep dog, is a round cotton ball, stained and dirty,
    that pops off the shelf and bounces in my way as I open the door.
And I am the wood and glue which hold us all together with my love.

Belinda

Fifth of July

My family is an expired firecracker
    set off by the blowtorch of divorce. We lay
        scattered in many directions.
My father is the wick, badly burnt
    but still glowing softly.
My mother is the blackened paper fluttering down,
    blowing this way and that, unsure where to land.
My sister is the fallen, colorful parachute,
    lying in a tangled knot, unable to see the beauty she
        holds.
My brother is the fresh, untouched powder that
    was protected from the flame. And I,
I am the singed, outside papers, curled away
    from everything, silently cursing
        the blowtorch.

John

LESSON SIXTY-ONE: PERSONIFICATION

Objectives: The students will be able to

- Recognize personification.
- Write Poem 6 using personification.

Procedure:

I. PREWRITING:

A. Define the term *personification:* to give human characteristics to inanimate objects.

B. Have the students brainstorm a list on the blackboard of inanimate objects which could be personified. For example,

hockey puck	*birch tree*	*dandelion*	*pencil*
worm	*textbook*	*car*	*basketball*

C. Ask students to pick one object to work on as a class. Suppose they pick *rain.*

D. Next, place on the blackboard the sentence: *Things I could do if I were the rain.* Their brainstormed list might look like this:

1. tempt kids to play in my mud puddles
2. postpone picnics
3. melt wicked witches
4. leave behind a rainbow
5. tap against the roof tops
6. paint the grass green

E. Explain that this list can now be shaped into a poem called "Things to Do If You're the Rain."

II. DRAFTING:
Encourage students to pick their own object, brainstorm a list of things they can do if they are that object, and shape the list into a poem.

Other examples:

Things to Do If You're a Paper Bag

Tote a tasty lunch
Be a perky puppet
Hide a hideous face
Remember a phone number
Crouch under cooling cookies
Blow yourself up and
Burst!

Margaret

My Life as a Washing Machine

I . . . guzzle gallons of soapy
water,
Eat mounds of soiled and
smelly clothes,
Get indigestion from
socks and underwear,
Belch and Burp and
Vibrate until someone pumps
my stomach and takes
everything out
except one
red
sock.

David

III. **REVISING AND PRESENTING:** Encourage students to use alliteration and other figures of speech whenever possible. When the final draft is complete, ask them to share it with others, if possible, before turning it in to you.

LESSON SIXTY-TWO: IMAGERY

Objectives: The students will be able to
- Define and recognize images.
- Write image couplets as Poem 7.

Procedure:

I. **PREWRITING**
   A. Define *image:* a picture in the mind. A writer appeals to the senses and transfers pictures from his mind to that of the reader.
   B. Have students close their eyes and visualize a happy scene from their own childhoods. Have them jot down the details on scratch paper and then go around the room asking each person to give the details of the memory so the rest of the class can "see" it. Explain that the scenes they are describing are also called *images* and as writers they should work to put images into their poetry.
   C. Write samples of image couplets on the blackboard.

   Did you ever see a turtle?
   Safely shelled, cautiously creeping, car target.

   Did you ever smell a December morning?
   Snow bleaching, exhaust stinging, smoke perfuming, wind whitening dawn.

   Have you heard a December morning?
   A feet crunching, wind moaning, car rumbling, furnace grinding day.

   Did you ever taste liver?
   Rubbery paper in cooked glue, fuzzy mold "good for you."

II. **DRAFTING**
   A. Have students create several couplets of their own based on this structure:
      Line 1 Did you ever feel/taste/see/hear/smell (choose one) _____ ?
      Line 2 Details which create and evoke an image
   B. Encourage students to create several couplets, using a variety of senses and unusual sense and noun combinations. For example, "Did you ever hear a sunset?" or "Did you ever taste a temper tantrum?"

III. **REVISING AND PRESENTING:** Have students write on unlined paper and if time allows, ask them to share their poems with the class before submitting their final drafts.

LESSON SIXTY-THREE: CHILDHOOD POEM

Objective: The students will be able to

- Write an extended Poem 8 using imagery, simile, metaphor, alliteration, or onomatopoeia.

Procedure:

I. PREWRITING

A. Read some or all of the following directions as the students brainstorm on their own paper for ideas and memories from their childhood.
1. Recall one of your favorite school activities from early grade school. Why was it a favorite? Get to a "once."
2. Recall something that frightened you. Explain briefly. Get to a "once."
3. Name something you did to tease a brother or sister.
4. Recall a favorite day or a favorite time of day. What made it special?
5. Recall your favorite pet. Why was it special?
6. Recall a favorite toy.
7. Recall a time you were lost.
8. Recall a favorite game.
9. Recall a special friend.
10. Recall a secret fear.
11. Recall a favorite dessert or candy.
12. Recall an older person who was special to you. Why?
13. What was the worst nightmare you ever had?
14. What was the best present you ever got?
15. What was the worst present you ever got?
16. How did you spend the Fourth of July?
17. Recall something special about the bedroom you had as a child.
18. Recall something special you wanted for a long time.

B. Have the students write a poem using some of the images from their brainstormed list to define their own childhood. Repeat the phrase "I remember" or "Childhood is." Encourage the students to keep these brainstorming lists for their next poems.

C. Distribute **Samples of Childhood Poems.**

II. DRAFTING: If time permits, encourage students to write two poems using both poetic structures.

III. REVISING AND PRESENTING: When students have revised and shaped their poems and written a completed copy on unlined paper, encourage them to read aloud. Point out that their poems truly do define and make us see a part of their childhoods.

8.7 Samples of Childhood Poems

I Remember

I remember playing on the swing at Grandma's
         and having "tea" with hot chocolate and
         toast.
    I remember riding on the tractor with Dad,
         his arm wrapped tightly around me, while I
         watch the plow churning behind me.
    I remember a green ski jacket and a red pair of skis.
    I remember praying, "Now I lay me down to sleep."
    I remember bringing home a gray kitten and Mom
         saying, "Get rid of that thing,"
         but keeping it anyway.
  And
    I remember getting sick on cold lemonade and
         crabapples.

                     Liz

Imagination

Childhood is being so scared to dive off the diving board
    that you sit on the end of it for five minutes
    crying.
Childhood is making snow-angels in a purple parka
    and having snow up your sleeves.
Childhood is a stuffed puppy carried everywhere.
Childhood is jumping into bed from the middle of the room
    so the gorilla underneath doesn't grab you.
Childhood is making sure all of your stuffed animals
    are in bed with you
        and waking up alone.

              Margaret

LESSON SIXTY-FOUR: EXTENDED POEM

Objective: The students will be able to

• Practice all their poetic skills in an extended poem (Poem 9).

Procedure:

I. PREWRITING

A. Ask the students to continue to brainstorm for ideas and memories on the brainstorming sheet they began in the last lesson. You may want to read additional directions such as the following:
   1. Recall several sounds from your childhood.
   2. Recall a smell that you hated. Why? (Locate it.)
   3. Recall a smell that you liked. Why?
   4. Recall something a parent did over and over again, a habit.
   5. Recall a place you used to go to be alone.
   6. Recall an expression an adult used over and over.
   7. Recall one of your favorite pieces of clothing. What made it special?
   8. Recall a time you got in trouble.
   9. Recall a dream you had over and over.
   10. Recall how far you were allowed to go alone. What were the limits of your neighborhood?
   11. Recall something you used to believe as a child (but don't anymore).

B. Write the following structure on the blackboard and explain it.
   1. Whenever I   see/smell/hear (choose one)
   2. It is   place/time (choose one)
      (Allow this to trigger a chain of memories—let it drift away from the original images.)
   3. But that is not my story. (back to original image)
   4. My story is: (add new, surprising detail)

C. Distribute the accompanying **Samples of Extended Poems** for students to examine.

II. DRAFTING: Confer with students as they work independently.

III. REVISING AND PRESENTING: When students have completed their poems and if time allows, have them gather in small groups to read, react, and offer suggestions to one another before they make their final copy and share their poem with others. Collect final copies.

8.8 Samples of Extended Poems

Memories

Whenever I smell
honeysuckle or sickbeds,
it is North Dakota in August,
and I am on the front porch
rocking in Grandpa's black chair,
reading *Huckleberry Finn,* and
eating chocolate chip cookies.

The wheat trucks rumble past,
and the whirling dust squeezes
through the window panes.

But this is not my story. My story is
grandparents in hospital beds
in the living room
dying
summer after summer
while I read on the porch and
wish myself away.

Mary

Baseball

Whenever I smell
  hot dogs,
it is mid-July in Boston,
  and I am
  on my father's shoulders,
  watching a baseball game
  and wearing a Red Sox hat.
  I reach for a foul ball
  and miss.

But that is not my story.
My story is my brother
  who can reach the ball
  and does
  and trades it
  for a
  hot dog.

Mike

LESSON SIXTY-FIVE: INVENTING LANGUAGE

Objective: The students will be able to

• Write Poem 10 emphasizing invented language, tone, mood, and onomatopoeia.

Procedure:

I. PREWRITING

A. Ask students to begin brainstorming on paper by listing some of their favorite words.

B. Read ten to twelve poems aloud. Explain to the students that you wish them to listen while you read and pick out and write down words from the poems that appeal to them. (They should work for a quantity.)

C. Keep reading until students have fifteen to twenty words on their papers.

D. Ask each student to contribute one of the words from his or her list while you write suggested words on the board. The blackboard list may look like this:

Phillipsburg	*purified*	*steps*	*skull*
hemlock	*twilight*	*striding*	*blooms*
quilted	*unpeeled*	*processed*	*silence*
mysterious	*arrested*	*bushes*	*bunched*
exotic	*bubble*	*wonder*	*fog*
quilted	*darkness*	*gentle*	*lives*
darkness	*clunks*	*wondrous*	*petal*

E. Ask the students to begin pairing the words which have been listed on the board in new and unusual combinations. Students may suggest combinations such as these:

bubble silence	*wondrous silence*
wonder steps	*processed darkness*
processed silence	*fog bushes*
striding silence	*unpeeled twilight*
fog silence	*petal steps*

II. DRAFTING

A. Have students work independently with their own lists of words, pairing words in as many combinations as possible.

B. In poem 10 the students use the words from their own lists, especially the word combinations, and arrange and shape them in new

231

ways. The invented combinations become a new language for expressing a mood or emotion, emphasizing the sounds of the words in combination. Distribute **Samples of Invented Language Poems.**

III. **REVISING:** Confer with individual students.

IV. **PRESENTING:** When final drafts are completed, ask students to volunteer to read aloud. Collect all drafts.

8.9 Samples of Invented Language Poems

CITY SILENCE

not striding clunks
not processed darkness
instead
the fog bushes petal step
into unpeeled twilight
and
bloom in Phillipsburg.

Jason

I SAW A LYING ANGEL

near my feet at twilight.
I knew
she woke me to die.
I heard a cry from a rose
as she crushed it into bone perfume.
The poison whistled
as it fell like fire down my throat.
I felt a train trembling
down its tracks as a traveler threw
hisses at people, barely visible in
the darkness.
The wind tossed a pebble
making it sing in the night.
The leaves shivered in a snapshot of fear
as I perished in the perfumed darkness.

Nancy

DREAM SNAPSHOTS

The dream snapshots
are full of
quilted colors
and crushed dust

Evening remembers
lilac truths
and hemlock hills

Leaves remember
half-shaven roses
mourning vistas
and heaven's footsteps

As stray cats sing
of exotic swans
and angel roses

Carl

LESSON SIXTY-SIX: HYPERBOLE

Objective: The students will be able to

- Write Poem 11 based on delightful lies or hyperbole.

Procedure:

I. PREWRITING

A. Explain *hyperbole:* an extravagant statement, not intended to be taken literally. "To wait an eternity" or "laugh until he was blue in the face" are examples. Go around the room, having students think of other similar expressions. For example, "She was so strong, she could bounce Paul Bunyan on her lap."

B. Explain to students the poem they will write on this day will be based on hyperbole or delightful lies.

C. Ask students: "When your parents were angry with you when you were little, what was their response? What lines or phrases did you come to expect from them?" Go around the room and ask each student to give an example.

D. Have students brainstorm on their papers for several more phrases. A list might look like this:

> *I've a good mind to . . .*
> *What am I going to do with you?*
> *Just wait until your father gets home!*
> *Don't you ever listen?*

E. Ask students to brainstorm again. This time ask them to list at least five things they really did as children that made their parents angry.

F. Ask students to list once more. This time they are to list at least five "terrible" things they wished they could have done as a child but didn't quite dare. Encourage them to exaggerate wildly.

G. Hand out and read together the accompanying **Sample of Hyperbole Poem.**

II. DRAFTING:
Explain that one phrase from their first list becomes the refrain of the poem and is repeated between stanzas. The stanzas are a mixture of truth and exaggerations.

III. REVISING AND PRESENTING:
Encourage students to try for three or four stanzas. Suggest they keep their verbs in present tense to maintain a sense of immediacy and speed. Collect final copies when all sharing and editing is completed.

8.10 Sample of Hyperbole Poem

Behave!

Takes careful aim on the fluffy
chickadee, squeezes the trigger on his
air rifle slowly, listens to the smack
of the pellet hitting its body, watches
the tiny gray feathers float lazily

down.

Can't you ever behave yourself?
    I have a mind to . . .

Sneaks up on the cat sleeping soundly on
the deck, raises the Glass Plus bottle
filled with cold water, gives the content
cat an icy shower.

Can't you ever behave yourself?
    I have a mind to . . .

Dashes into kitchen, bangs open the
refrigerator door, heaves the milk
and baby food to the floor, bites
the baby's arm and runs outside.

Can't you ever behave yourself?
    I have a mind to . . .

Toys with the handle of the hockey stick,
Swings it violently at the sheet of glass,
listens to the broken pieces tinkle to the
floor of the old cabin, and smiles

happily.

Can't you ever behave yourself?
    I have a mind to . . .

Terry

LESSON SIXTY-SEVEN: VOICE

Objective: The students will be able to

- Write Poem 12 emphasizing the speaking voice.

Procedure:

    I. **PREWRITING**
- A. The one-sentence poem is the last poem in the unit and one of the most enjoyable for the students. Explain they will again be writing about a memory. Suggest they review previous brainstorming lists. As a refresher, ask them to respond to the following additional directions.
  1. Recall a time you were embarrassed.
  2. Recall a time you were punished.
  3. Recall a time you were sad.
- B. Distribute, read, and discuss **Samples of One Sentence Poems**.
- C. Have students choose one memory and zero in on its details, jotting down more ideas on a brainstorming list or a cluster.

  II. **DRAFTING:** Ask the students to freewrite about the incident for as long as necessary. Encourage them to become the young child they once were and to write in their young voice.

 III. **REVISING:** Explain the poem is to be only one sentence although it may be nearly a page in length.
- A. Because it can be only one sentence, many "ands" will have to be added. (These are useful because they serve to make the speaker sound young and breathless.)
- B. Suggest the writers insert phrases and language they might have used when they were the age of the memory.
- C. Ask the writers to edit, adding repetitive elements (words, phrases, or unusual capitalization) to give the poem structure.

 IV. **PRESENTING:** When the poems are completely revised and edited, have students read them aloud before turning in their final copies.

Note: You may decide to have the students collect all their poems in personal booklets of poetry. See Lesson Seventy-five for directions and suggestions.

8.11 Samples of One-Sentence Poems

Mud

One day in first grade our teacher Miss McKennet
who had never been married because she was mean
(and my mom said she should never have been a
teacher anyway) told us we could not go outside to
play because it was **muddy,** and everyone would
get all **dirty** and get just everything **dirty,** but
me and George went outside across the street to
play anyway (which we weren't supposed to do
because of all the cars that went by that street
let alone even being outside cause of all the
mud), but anyway, Miss McKennet must've seen us
out her window (which was cracked from when
Tom shot it with a BB gun and had to wash desks
for two weeks), and she came out to get us so we
threw **mud** at her and ran, but it was no good
cause she caught us both and dragged us back to
homeroom which was filled with **clean** kids
playing quietly, and she turned to me and pulled
down my pants and gave me a spanking, and then
she went after George, but he got away and never
did get spanked in front of all his friends.

Harry

Recess

I used to get chased by a gang of girls in first grade, and **I hated it,** because
I was outnumbered 5 to 1, and I didn't stand a chance against them, and my
heart would always beat thump, thump, thump when Ms Klingensmith let us
go outside for recess, and I would always be the first one out because I
wanted to get a good hiding place so those girls wouldn't chase me, or I
would run to the swings and swing high and higher, and I would feel free,
but that didn't work, because they would wait until I got tired, and they'd
wrestle me to the ground and start tickling me, and they wouldn't let me go
'til I said **I love you** to them, but I would get away, and they would chase me
around the school, but after awhile they would quit, and one time when we
all got in class, Marilyn chased me into the musty coat closet and I couldn't
do nothing because she was bigger 'n me, and she wrestled me to the floor
and started kissing me with the lights out, and **I liked it.**

Tim

Beautiful

I am five, and I have to have my hair put in bristle
curlers for a wedding, and mom shoves the picks in
really hard, and I hate sleeping on those bristle
things cuz my hair has gotten yanked and pulled
back until I got chinese eyes, and I can't sleep cuz I
feel like a billion needles are poking me, and in the
morning the curlers are ratted and snarled, and
mom pulls and yanks until they finally come
loose, and that's the part I hate the most about bristle
curlers.

Lisa

unit 9

WRITING AND PUBLISHING

In Lessons Sixty-eight to Seventy-five students are asked to return to prose after completing the poetry unit. The quality of the writing which occurs after the poetry unit is high and well worth the time. The young writers have become more sensitive to word choices, economy, repetition, and figures of speech and use these elements more effectively and naturally in their subsequent writing.

In this unit students are asked to freewrite twice on separate days. They choose one of their two freewritings to revise extensively and share with the group. One suggestion for a topic is generally a safe one while the second encourages some risk taking. This approach is repeated and results in five freewritings and three revisions. If you wish for students to carry all three revisions through the entire writing process, the time required for the entire unit is several weeks. Complete directions are also included for publishing students' collected writings.

LESSON SIXTY-EIGHT: FREEWRITING

Objective: The students will be able to

- Practice writing freely using poetic elements in prose in Freewriting 19.

Procedure:

  I. **PREWRITING:** Introduce Freewriting 19.

    A. Explain to students the suggested topic: an animal or a pet.

    B. Read or distribute the accompanying **Student Sample.**

    C. Read the following brainstorming directions for students to respond to in writing:
- 1. List the pets you have had.
- 2. Have you ever had any unusual pets? A gerbil, a turtle, a mouse, for example. A classroom pet?
- 3. Think about an unusual experience in which an animal played a part.
- 4. Which was your favorite pet? Why?
- 5. Which was your least favorite pet? Why?
- 6. Zero in on one of these animals. List as many details about it as possible:
  - a. Did it have a name?
  - b. If you owned the animal, how did you get it?
  - c. What made it special or unique?
  - d. Think about *one time* concerning the pet. Jot down as many details as possible about this time.
  - e. Make a cluster or visualize a particular incident.

  II. **DRAFTING** Freewriting 19: A sample direction:

For the remainder of the period write freely about an animal or pet or a topic of your own.

9.1 Student Sample

In a Stand of Pines

The truck bounces as we drive down Birchmont from the vet's office toward our house. The radio is off, but mom and I don't talk. I fidget with my seatbelt and look nervously back at the cardboard box lying in the bed of the truck. As we reach our driveway, the motor whines as mom downshifts. She turns cautiously and drives toward the open garage. The crumbling tar driveway is covered with twigs and clumps of green leaves blown from the trees during the previous night's storm. The truck glides silently into the dark garage.

We undo our seat belts, get out, and go to the back of the truck. I bite at my thumbnail as mom opens the back door of the truck; the tailgate opens with a thud, and mom slides the box onto it. She lifts the lid from the box and slowly pulls away the green towel. Jenny lies curled with her paws to her chest. Her eyes are closed, but a blue tongue hangs from her open mouth Mom cautiously strokes our pet's head. I am scared and sad at the death of our only cat, but the idea of death makes me curious, too, and I move closer to the open box and reach out to touch Jenny. Her body is hard. The only sounds I hear in the garage are the rhythmic ticking of the cooling engine and my own breathing.

Mom closes the box and clears her throat. "Dave, why don't you get a spade?" I walk slowly to the garage wall and grab a rusty shovel from its hook. When I return, mom is cradling the box. She leads the way down the bleached cement steps and toward the woods. I drag the shovel through the wet grass. The sky is full of gray clouds heavy with rain. They move fast in the July wind, and bright rays of sunlight flare between the clouds. We follow the path until we reach a thick stand of pines and birch. "This looks okay, Dave."

I stab the spade into the black dirt and scoop clumps away. The wind blows harder now, and the smell of rain filters through the trees. Raindrops begin to fall. The hole reaches the appropriate size, and I look to mom. She nods and hands me the box. I place it into the grave and begin covering it. Each clod of dirt falls with a hollow thud. The rain lets up, and as I shape the top of the mound with my hands, it stops. I rise and wipe my hands on my jeans. We stand beside the grave as sunlit filters through the green, dripping leaves. "The sun's shining, Mom," I tell her. She looks at me and smiles a bit. I pick up the spade, and we walk together toward the house.

David

LESSON SIXTY-NINE: FREEWRITING

Objective: The students will be able to

• Practice writing freely in Freewriting 20.

Procedure:

I. **PREWRITING:** Introduce Freewriting 20.

    A. Explain to students the suggested topic: a time they grew up quickly.

    B. Read or distribute the accompanying **Student Samples.**

    C. The first decades of our lives is a growing up time. Usually we mature gradually. At other times we encounter an incident or episode which causes us to grow up a bit more quickly. These incidents may be as simple as buying a bottle of ketchup on our own or as serious as literally being on our own in a new country.

    D. Ask the students to think of some times like this in their own lives and brainstorm on paper in response to the following directions.

        1. Where are you in your family order? First child? Middle? Last?

        2. List some responsibilities your parents have given you?

        3. Have you ever worked for someone else? Think about some difficult times "on the job."

        4. Think about something you faced which was difficult? Why was it difficult? How did you handle it? What did you learn about yourself?

        5. Think about some of your accomplishments?

        6. Zero in on one time.

        7. Visualize this time and jot down as many details about it as possible.

II. **DRAFTING** Freewriting 20: A sample direction.

For the remainder of the class period, write freely about a time you grew up quickly, or pick a topic of your choice.

9.2 Student Samples

Shopping

My mom would never let me go to the store by myself when I was small. Instead, she always sent me with one of my older sisters. I remember getting so angry when she would say, "I need somebody to go to the store," and I always came running, saying, "I will, I will," but she would always say, "No, you're too young."

There was one time, though, that was special. I was the only child home, and she needed a bottle of ketchup. She said, "Connie, I need you to go to the store." My heart was thumping when I followed her into the house. She put the money in my pocket and a note in my hand and told me to give it to the lady behind the counter.

At the store I waited in line and followed mom's directions. The lady behind the counter put my ketchup in a bag and smiled at me. I went out of the store feeling happy and proud, but when I got in back of the store, the bag slipped and fell to the ground with a crash. I just sat on the ground and cried and cried. The lady from the store found me there. "Don't cry," she said, and led me back to the store. I gave her my change, and she put another bottle into a new bag.

When I got home I told mom the truth, but she only smiled and said, "This has happened to your older sisters, too. You did a good job, and I'm proud of you."

Connie

Looking Back

Before 1980, I was a happy boy. All I had to do was go to school. I worried about nothing and had no responsibilities. After 1980, I was still happy, but by then I could see how bad the communism was in my country, Viet Nam.

One day my parents spoke with me. My father said, "You're going to leave our country. It is for your future." I was surprised. I had lived with my family all my life, and now I was being sent away from them. I didn't want to go and told my father that. He said, "Grow up, boy!"

When I got into the boat to leave the country, I realized I was going to have to grow up. I spent seven days in a boat, and no one worried about me. The people around me took care of their own families, but I was alone. I felt sorry for myself when I saw some of the boys my own age call to their parents, "Dad, Mom, I am thirsty. Give me some water," while I was getting water for myself. I wished my parents were there.

When we arrived in Indonesia, everything was new to me. I told myself, "Hey, boy, you are on your own. Life isn't going to be as easy as you think. Be careful in everything you do."

After a few days on the island, I was interviewed. I was surprised that I did all of the talking with no trouble. They even asked me the question, "How many children do you have?" Gee, how could I have children when I was only sixteen? I told myself, "Tun, now you'll really find out how life is. Just stay calm." And that is what I did.

Tun

LESSON SEVENTY: REVISING, EDITING, AND PRESENTING

Objective: The students will be able to

- Revise Freewriting 19 or 20 and present it to the large circle as Revision 8.

Procedure:

This lesson may take at *least seven class periods* if you decide to have the students complete the entire writing process.

Day One:	Students choose between Freewriting 19 or 20 and revise the writing in any way necessary to present in the small circle on the following day.
Day Two:	Students conduct peer conferences in the small circle.
Day Three:	Students make additional revisions taking into account recommendations made in peer conferences and student-teacher conferences.
Day Four:	Students edit independently for mechanical correctness and proofread in pairs.
Day Five:	Students complete a final draft of Revision 8.
Days Six and Seven:	Students read the final drafts in the large circle. A copy of the revision may be saved for publication at the end of this unit. (If necessary, papers are graded at this time.)

An option for students who choose to rework the writing about a pet: Suggest they revise it as a children's story (for a particular age group).

LESSON SEVENTY-ONE: FREEWRITING

Objective: The students will be able to

- Practice writing freely in Freewriting 21.

Procedure:

I. **PREWRITING:** Introduce Freewriting 21.
- A. Explain to the students the suggested topic: a time in their lives when they felt badly about themselves; a time they felt like a nothing, a nobody; or a time when someone else was made to feel this way.
- B. Read or distribute copies of the **Student Samples.**
- C. Point out to the students that we all have experiences like the ones described by these students. The following brainstorming directions may help them get started:
   1. Think about a time someone was angry with you.
   2. Think about a time you tried unsuccessfully to do something.
   3. Think about a time you couldn't do something as well as someone else.
   4. Think about a time you felt embarrassed.
   5. Think about a time you saw someone else being picked on.
   6. Zero in on one of these incidents and list all the details.

II. **DRAFTING** Freewriting 20: A sample direction.
For the remainder of the class period, write freely about a time you felt badly about yourself or saw someone else being made to feel badly (or pick a topic of your own choice).

9.3 Student Samples

Failing

One time in seventh grade, soon after I'd moved to Thief River Falls, I was third chair in band, so I decided to challenge Jim, who had first chair. I practiced a piece over and over, and I thought I had a pretty good chance of winning a higher chair.

On the day of the challenge I was nervous but confident because all the girls I knew were wishing me good luck and were saying, "Oh, you'll win!" By the time I got to the band room, I felt pretty sure of myself. I played the song and made a few mistakes, but I thought I had done pretty well. Jim went into the band room when I came out, and I could hear his playing through the door. Soon he made a mistake and stopped playing. By this time I was sure I "had it made."

When my teacher finally came out of the room, I waited for him to smile and congratulate me. Instead, he said, "I'm sorry, Lee Ann, we'll keep the same seating arrangement."

I was too stunned to say anything. I numbly put my clarinet away and started home. No one was home when I got there, and I just ran down to the basement and cried.

                                                                          Lee Ann

Kool Aid

I was seven years old, and it was a hot summer day. I complained about having nothing to do, and my mom finally suggested I go to the corner and sell Kool Aid. It was a great idea, something I loved to do. In fact, I had even built a special stand to sell it in the summer before.

I made the Kool Aid myself, got the cups, and put the stand on the corner. My stand was white with a couple of boards missing. The rest of it was crooked, but I had done it all myself and was proud of it. I was in business!

Sometime later that afternoon, my Aunt Amy walked over to me and bought a glass saying, "This better be good." I thought she was joking and I smiled. Suddenly, she spit out the Kool Aid. "This is horrible. Don't you know how to make Kool Aid yet. No wonder you don't get more customers. This stand is a piece of junk!"

She dumped the Kool Aid on the ground and went into the house to make some more. When she came out she brought my sister's flowered play table. She threw my stand into a pile of leaves and set me in front of the table. "There. Now maybe you'll sell something," and she left.

I don't think I ever sold Kool Aid after that day.

                                                                          Tim

LESSON SEVENTY-TWO: FREEWRITING

Objective: The students will be able to

- Practice writing freely in Freewriting 22.

Procedure:

  I. **PREWRITING:** Introduce Freewriting 22.
- A. Explain to students the suggested topic: an incident from their childhoods which wasn't funny at the time but now, in looking back, is funny. Encourage them to emphasize the humor as they write.
- B. Read or distribute the accompanying **Student Sample.**
- C. Ask the students to recall incidents from their own childhoods. The following brainstorming directions will help them get started:
  1. Think of a time you got in trouble.
  2. Think of a time you were in danger.
  3. Think of some stories your family tells about you as a child.
  4. Think of something you did that was foolish.
  5. Zero in on one incident and list as many of its details as possible.

 II. **DRAFTING** Freewriting 21: A sample direction.

Write about an incident from your childhood that wasn't funny at the time but, in looking back, is. Emphasize the humor.

9.4 Student Sample

I Stuck Out My Tongue

When I was in kindergarten, my family lived in Blaine, Minnesota, and I went to Jefferson Elementary School. The principal's name was Mr. Quincher, but we all called him "Mr. Cruncher" because he was mean. On the first day of school, he called an assembly and read us the rules. "Anyone who runs in the halls will be brought to me. Anyone who . . . ." Then he held up his big green paddle and slapped it against his podium, SMACK, and said, "I'll spank you if I have to." Then he dismissed his wide-eyed students to their classrooms.

One winter day we were on the playground. I was playing on the jungle gym. As I climbed higher, right in front of me was a bar. I'm not sure why, but I stuck my tongue out, and it stuck to the metal. Wow! Was it stuck.

I looked around for help, but could only see Linda Jansen. "Hey, Mike, watcha doin', kissin' the pipe?"

I tried to say, "No I got my tongue stuck on the bar, but it came out, "Mo, in gob me ton thock on da baa."

Linda thought I had sworn at her, and she ran off crying, "Teacher, Teacher."

Well, I was in a fix. I thought, "What if the teacher believes Linda. Off I'll go to Mr. Cruncher with his big green paddle. Smack." I saw Micky coming. "Hey, Icky, ma ton ith thock on do naa." (Hey, Micky, my tongue is stuck on the bar.) "How boo lh gib it oth?" (How do I get it off?)

"Just pull it off."

"Buh dat ill hurt." (But that will hurt.)

"Well, that's the only way I know," Micky shouted.

So . . . I pulled it off and, wow, it did hurt.

At least I didn't have to visit Mr. Cruncher's office, but my tongue hurt for a long time.

Mike

LESSON SEVENTY-THREE: REVISING, EDITING, AND PRESENTING

Objective: The students will be able to

- Revise Freewritings 21 or 22 and present to the circle as Revision 9.

Procedure:

This lesson may take at least *seven class periods,* if you plan to have the students take the writing through the entire writing process.

Day One:	Students choose between Freewriting 21 and 22 and revise a draft in any way necessary to present to the small circle on the following day. Encourage students to use all their self-editing skills.
Day Two:	Students work together in peer conferences and confer with you.
Day Three:	Students revise independently taking into account recommendations from their peers and from you.
Day Four:	Students edit for mechanical correctness and proofread in pairs.
Day Five:	Students complete a final copy of Revision 9.
Days Six and Seven:	Students read final drafts aloud in the large circle. Final drafts may be saved for publication at the end of this unit. (If necessary, papers are graded at this time.)

LESSON SEVENTY-FOUR: THE COMPLETE WRITING PROCESS

Objective: The students will be able to

- Practice writing freely in Freewriting 23 and carry the writing through the entire writing process as Revision 10.

Procedure:

This lesson takes the student through the entire writing process and may require *up to eight class periods.*

Day One:

I. **PREWRITING:** Introduce Freewriting 23.

   A. An ideal option for the last lesson in this unit is to suggest that students choose their own topics independently or pick an earlier freewriting or journal entry to expand and carry through the entire process.

   B. Another option is to suggest a broad topic such as, write about your parents' philosophy in raising you. Focus on an incident or incidents which you believe are representative of how you have been raised.

   C. Be sure students understand this writing will undergo the entire writing process and will be shared in the small and large circles.

   D. Read or distribute copies of **Student Sample.**

   E. Ask the students who plan to write about their parents' philosophy to think about incidents which might be representative of how their parents raised them. (Many students enjoy this topic. However, because there may be families or students who are not comfortable with it, be sure to emphasize free choice of topics.)

   The following brainstorming directions will be helpful:

   1. List some of your family's priorities.
   2. List some of the rules you "live by."
   3. List a punishment you might expect if you break a rule.
   4. List some lessons a parent or guardian has taught you.
   5. Focus on specific incidents and list as many details as possible.

II. **DRAFTING** Freewriting 23: A sample direction.

   For the remainder of the class period write about your parents' philosophy in raising you. Write about an incident (or several) which are representative of this philosophy. Feel free to choose another topic if you wish.

250

Day Two:	Students revise independently.
Day Three:	Students confer in peer groups.
Day Four:	Students revise independently in response to suggestions from their peers and from you.
Day Five:	Students edit for mechanical correctness and proofread in pairs.
Day Six:	Students produce a final, well-edited draft.
Days Seven and Eight:	Students read final drafts in the large circle. Copies may be saved for publication at the end of this unit.

9.5 Student Sample

Sharing

"Oh, nice puppy, she's my puppy and she loves me!" said the five-year-old my mom was babysitting that steamy, summer day.

"She's not your dog," I informed her. "She lives here at my house, and this isn't your house." I was eight and not very tolerant of this kid.

"Sometimes this is my house."

"No, it's not."

"Un huh!"

"Shut up," I shouted.

"Kim, will you come in here."

"Oh, oh," I thought. Mom had heard us fighting. I knew that I was in the right. She was wrong. Missy was my dog, and this was my house.

"Kim, Andrea is just little and you should stop teasing her. She's a guest in our house today, and you should treat her like one."

"But Mom, she said that our dog was . . . ."

"That's enough. Now go out there and be nice. Understand?"

I walked into the living room and found Andrea sitting in the recliner hugging Missy. "She loves me. Oh, Missy, you are my dog aren't you?" she taunted.

Kim

LESSON SEVENTY-FIVE: PUBLISHING

Objective: The students will be able to

- Collect all ten revisions and any extra writings and publish in a personal booklet.

Procedure:

This lesson may take *three or more class periods*.

I. PUBLISHING
   A. Make available construction paper, colored pens, paste, and a stapler.
   B. Return all final drafts to students.
   C. Ask the students to organize their best writings in a booklet which will contain the following:
      1. Decorated front cover.
      2. Title page—have students consult published books as models.
      3. Table of contents.
      4. Revisions and/or poetry and any additional writings.
      5. Illustrations (if the students wish).
      6. Back cover, which contains an "About the Author" section. This section is placed on the inside of the cover alongside the right margin.
         a. Students study similar sections in published books.
         b. They write "About the Author" in third person. This section may include:
            (1) Date of birth and birthplace.
            (2) Description of their family.
            (3) Past achievements.
            (4) Hobbies and interests.
            (5) Work history.
            (6) Goals and plans for the future.
         c. Encourage students to include a photograph or a cartoon sketch of themselves in this section.
   D. You may hesitate to make this assignment to older students. Don't trust this feeling. Your students will be as pleased with the product as younger students are. Publishing allows them time to organize and save writings they already prize.
   E. If possible, do not grade the books, but do collect and read them quickly, making comments on removable paper on self-sticking notes about stories or poems you particularly like. (If there are writings you would like to use as samples for students in other classes, this is the time to ask for copies.)

Another option: Ask each student to copy and contribute one writing to a class booklet which is duplicated for everyone and read in the large circle. (You may wish to limit each student to one page.)

II. This is also a good time for a final conference with each student. Ask students to pick one of their revisions. **A Checklist for Student-Teacher Conferences** accompanies this lesson, and both the student and teacher respond to it. This is also one of the times a grade may be given. One option for grading is to have students submit one of their first polished revisions along with a second they feel is an example of their best writing. A grade may be given which reflects the student's growth as a writer.

Name _____ Date _____

9.6 Checklist for Student-Teacher Conference

The student answers
yes or *no*

The teacher answers
agree or *disagree*

_____ 1. The beginning of the writing is effective. _____

_____ 2. The shape or organization of the paper works well. _____

_____ 3. The writing makes the reader "see." _____

_____ 4. The writing uses specific words. _____

_____ 5. The writing is economical. _____

_____ 6. The ending of the paper works well. _____

_____ 7. The title is inviting to a reader and offers a clue to the point of the paper. _____

_____ 8. Strong verbs are used. _____

_____ 9. Direct dialogue is included. _____

_____ 10. The paper affects the reader in some way. _____

_____ 11. The paragraphing is appropriate. _____

_____ 12. The paper has been edited for spelling, capitalization, and punctuation. _____

Additional Comments: Additional Comments:

APPENDIX A

DESIGNING ADDITIONAL WRITING ASSIGNMENTS

1. Design or revise any assignment so that it fits your own teaching style and is appropriate for a particular group of students. You may need to take some risks and try some unfamiliar techniques, but you also should feel comfortable with the approach. Many teaching styles work well, and many personality types teach writing well.

2. Try a particular writing before asking your own students to do it. In addition to providing an example for students, this will help you analyze the steps in the process and foresee any problems or concerns inherent in the exercise.

3. Choose ideas which appeal to the common experience of students but allow diversity and individual responses. Writing experiences should focus on what students do know rather than on what they don't know. Many students believe their lives are dull in comparison to what they see in movies or television. Many will say, "Nothing important has ever happened to me." In addition, many classroom experiences also emphasize what students don't yet know. Help them recognize that their lives are filled with an enormous amount of material to draw on. Try focusing on ordinary, even mundane moments, such as walking along a beach or waiting for a school bus.

4. Offer a variety of writing experiences. While many students write easily about subjects based on emotion, others never do. Some students need clear boundaries; others do not. Offer some exercises based on prescribed forms and others which are open-ended.

5. Keep in mind the diverse learning styles of students. Provide suggestions and alternatives for students who don't easily see a variety of choices. Provide models for those who learn best from them.

Ideas for Getting Started

PHOTOS OR ART PRINTS—Reproduced mass-media photos or prints are available as story starters. Actual photos students bring from home are probably more helpful to most students. (Students may exchange with others.)

MUSIC—Writing with music in the background is most effective when the music or sounds are unfamiliar. *Breathe* and *Petals* (by Marcus Allen and John Bernoff, Rising Sun Records, P.O. Box 524, Mill Valley, CA 94942) enables students to relax and provides a sense of solitude despite the classroom context.

SENSE DEPRIVATION—Ask students to wear blindfolds; then examine a collection of interesting tactile objects before writing.

SENSE STIMULATION—Bring air freshener (be aware of student allergies) or distribute pickles, lemons, or spices to smell and taste. This exercise can trigger memory writing.

FOUND OBJECTS
   A. Gather a tray of found objects. Let each person pick an item and examine it closely. Ask each to sketch his or her object prior to writing. This leads easily to

a poem emphasizing personification and the sketch may become an illustration for the final draft.

B. Ask students to collect newspaper headlines or overheard scraps of conversation. Then shape or arrange the lines as a poem to achieve a particular effect.

C. Give students a comic strip sequence with the language removed. Ask them to write a narrative with an emphasis on descriptive detail.

D. Use a short, factual newspaper article about something unusual or funny and have students imagine more of what happened, then write a story or play (or anything, really) about it.

TRANSLATIONS—Have students find human interest stories in newspapers and magazines and translate these into poems, television news reports, or editorials.

POINT OF VIEW—Ask students to take a single incident and describe it from several points of view. For example, a student arrives late for school. The writer may describe the incident from the student's viewpoint, from the teacher's viewpoint, or a parent's viewpoint. Another option is to have students write about one incident using different voices (first or third) or different modes (a note, poem, dialogue, or journal entry, for example).

COMBINATIONS—Have students write a series of freewritings to be combined, using the best of each in a final draft. For example, a description of a favorite childhood toy may begin as a memory writing. A second writing on the same topic may be a lost and found notice for the "lost" toy. A third exercise may be a description of the toy for someone who is blind. The final draft includes the best elements of all three writings.

APPENDIX B

WRITING IN LITERATURE CLASSES AND ACROSS THE CURRICULUM

The following are some of the successful ways teachers are finding to implement the writing process in literature classes.

READING JOURNALS

Students in literature classes are frequently asked to keep journals in which they respond in writing to reading assignments. The journal can help students understand textbook material. Often, students make connections between what they read and their own lives, connections they sometimes do not make in more formal writing assignments. The journal also allows students to make connections between various selections they have read. They frequently pay attention to writers' styles because the journal encourages students to read more carefully.

Teachers do not evaluate the journal for mechanics and usage. The entries, in essence, are rough drafts. However, teachers do respond to the content of the writing, pushing students to go beyond obvious or superficial comments and plot summary. Journals may be used as a basis for further student writing about topics found in the journals, topics which often deal with point of view, character analysis, or comparison and contrast. Students can also be asked to share entries with the class, and this frequently results in lively discussions because students have already done a great deal of thinking about the topic.

The following is a list of beginning sentences which are useful in helping students begin a reading journal:

1. I like/dislike this idea because . . .
2. This character reminds me of someone I know because . . .
3. This character reminds me of myself because . . .
4. This character is like [name of character] in [title of work] because . . .
5. I think this setting is important because . . .
6. This scene reminds me of a similar scene in . . .
7. I like/dislike this writing because . . .
8. This section is particularly effective because . . .
9. The ideas here remind me of the ideas in [title of work] because . . .
10. This incident reminds me of a similar situation in my own life. It happened when . . .

FREEWRITING

Asking students to freewrite in the literature class has all of the advantages of the journal and is far easier to administer. Class sets of journals are physically cumbersome, and the pressure of time on you is greater when students are expected to respond to assigned topics or particular pieces of literature which will be discussed on specific days. Journals have become so popular in many subject areas that there is also a danger of students being overwhelmed with journal assignments.

Suppose a class is reading and discussing Carson McCuller's short story, "Sucker." (The story describes a family relationship in which an older boy loses the love and respect of a younger cousin.) Decide which points are significant for a class discussion and fashion one or two topics which would give every student an opportunity to think and write about the ideas (and relate them to their own lives) before the actual class discussion begins. Two freewriting questions for this short story might be

1. Describe something you did as a youngster that was guaranteed to tease or anger a brother or sister or other family member.
2. In what way is what you did as a youngster like or unlike Pete's treatment of Sucker?

After students have written for approximately five minutes, collect the papers and quickly check the students' responses. You'll know immediately which students have a clear understanding of the story and which do not. In addition, you may pick one or two of the better writings to read anonymously. Students enjoy this. They like to hear the writing of their classmates, and having their own writing chosen to be read aloud is an immediate reward. Students also learn to comment about what they do not understand, and you will be able to respond to these questions at once. Because the students have been given time to write first, they have clarified their thinking and the ensuing class discussion is far more lively and more likely to involve all of the students.

In a longer unit, you might design freewriting questions for several pieces of literature which, when returned to the writer, constitute most of the prewriting necessary for a longer, more involved composition assignment covering an entire unit. Consider the following unit plan: The teacher asks students to read short stories having to do with family relationships. The teacher plans to have the students write a longer more formal composition later which compares the major characters.

The following are examples of stories which might be included in such a unit. Prewriting questions accompany each story, questions which are intended to help students understand the characterization of the mother in each story as well as to give them an opportunity to relate the story to their own lives.

STORY	FREE WRITING QUESTIONS
1. "Average Waves" by Anne Tyler (A mother places a retarded son in an institution.)	1. Discuss the reasons why the mother places her son in the institution. Was hers a selfish or unselfish act? Describe a time your parent gave up something for you.
2. "The Sky Is Gray" by Ernest J. Gaines (A mother "fathers" her son by teaching him to kill two birds because they have no food.)	2. Describe an important lesson your mother taught you. In what ways does the mother in this story teach her son "to be a man"?
3. Chapter One of *Growing Up* by	3. Describe a time your mother made

Russell Baker (A mother is determined to raise a son who will make
something of himself.)

you do something "for your own
good."
How is Russell's mother like yours?

Directions for a more extended writing assignment dealing with these stories
(which allows students to use their class freewritings as the prewriting) could then
logically be compare and contrast the mothers in the stories "Average Waves," "The
Sky Is Gray," and *Growing Up*. If you wish to give students an opportunity to respond
in a more personal way, you might add, "In what ways are these characters like or
different from your own mother?" Each writing assignment is geared to foster
thinking and understanding and each becomes useful again in a more extended
assignment. The teacher of literature may plan and design any writing assignment in
this manner.

THE COMPLETE WRITING PROCESS

Every student should understand the entire writing process so thoroughly that he or
she can use it appropriately in every circumstance. Essay questions are a favorite
means of testing in literature classes. If you expect students to write essay answers,
spend time teaching your students to write essay answers and to recognize the
relationship of the essay answer to the writing process. Help students understand the
four steps in writing an essay answer:

STEPS IN WRITING AN ESSAY ANSWER	STAGES OF THE WRITING PROCESS

1. Analyze the question.
  A. Circle all direction words such as *list, compare, trace,* or *describe*.
  B. Underline all key words.
  C. Determine the number of parts to the question.
	1. Prewriting

2. Develop ideas.
  A. Brainstorm or cluster.
  B. Jot a brief outline.
  C. Reread the question.
	2. Prewriting

3. Write out the answer.
  A. Restate the question as the first sentence of the answer.
  B. Freewrite, following the jot outline.
	3. Drafting

4. Polish the freewriting carefully, but do not recopy.	4. Revision

Students are frequently unsuccessful in writing essay answers because they too
often overlook the prewriting activities and begin drafting immediately. When they
come to realize that ideas are the main concern of this kind of writing, and if they
understand the writing process, they will spend more time analyzing what they are

being asked to do and brainstorming for ideas. Once these important prewriting activities are completed, essay answers become very much like freewritings, freewritings which are not recopied, but edited and polished sufficiently to communicate with the teacher as audience.

The following is a simple exercise which helps students practice writing essay answers:

1. Hand out two lemon drops to each student. (One is to eat immediately.)
2. Explain to the students they will practice writing an essay answer based on the following directions.

   Define and describe a lemon drop. Be sure to appeal to all five senses in your answer.
3. Ask students to identify the instruction words and circle them. (*Define, describe,* and *appeal*)
4. Have students identify and underline any other key words. (*lemon drop, five senses*)
5. Ask students to identify the number of parts to the question. (two)
6. Have students cluster or brainstorm for ideas. A cluster may look like this:

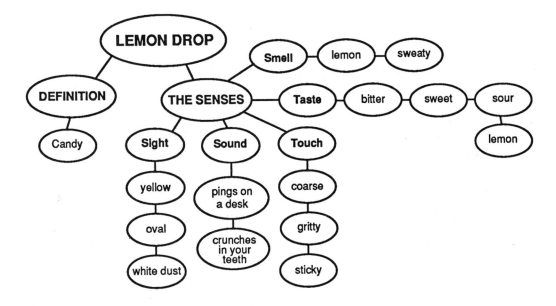

7. Have students number their brainstorming as a kind of jot outline.
8. Ask them to reread the question, then freewrite their answers using the cluster or jot outline as a guide.
9. After the freewriting is completed, have the students edit their original drafts. (Suggest they do not recopy an essay answer, but make legible and clear changes if necessary.)
10. Call on volunteers to read their trial essay answers aloud and make comments about them.

PEER CONFERENCES

Students writing in literature classes should also be given a chance to write and share early drafts of major writing assignments with teachers in conferences and with their peers in small groups. You can fashion a checklist to help students respond to one another's papers.

1. What do you like about the writing?
2. What questions do you have about the writing?
3. What suggestions do you have for improving the writing?

In later drafts, checklists emphasizing mechanical correctness may be added:

	line number
1. Are there capitalization errors?	_____
2. Are all sentences complete?	_____
3. Are all words spelled correctly?	_____
4. Are commas used correctly?	_____

AUDIENCE

It is helpful for students writing in a literature class to write for many audiences. It is well worth the class time to have students read final polished writings aloud to the class. Students may also be encouraged to submit writings to literary magazines, contests, and the school newspaper. There are other possible audiences, depending upon the particular writing assignment. If, for example, a class is studying literature about growing old in the twentieth century, a logical writing assignment would be for the students to interview and write personality profiles about elderly people they know. Community newspapers frequently feature sections such as "Looking Back" and are likely to welcome student writing about members of the community. It is also possible to have students publish their profiles in a class magazine or to have students deliver a final copy of the writing or class magazine to the subjects of the profiles.

EXPERIMENTATION

When students are studying a variety of forms or literary elements, it is helpful to expect them to experiment with the same elements in their own writing. Freewritings might be structured into simple short stories, for example. In addition, students might also be asked to experiment with the chronology of their stories by introducing flashbacks. Students studying point of view may be asked to change a first-person freewriting or journal entry to third person. They may also try converting a fictional piece to another point of view. After reading *To Kill a Mockingbird,* they might rewrite the mob scene, telling it from Tom's point of view or the Mrs. Dubose episode from Jem's point of view. If students are studying poetry, they may be expected to write poetry of their own. If they're studying drama, they may write dialogues or radio plays involving several characters.

VARIETY IN WRITING ASSIGNMENTS

Students in literature classes often respond positively to a wide variety of writing options. Rather than requiring a traditional character analysis, you might ask students to assume the role of one character in a piece of fiction to describe still another character. If students are reading a novel such as *Lord of the Flies,* you might ask them to describe one of the boys on the island from the **point of view** of another boy. Ralph, for example, would certainly describe Piggy differently than Jack would.

In place of traditional book reports, students may write letters about a book to the teacher or to a classmate. Encourage students to write (and mail) letters of review to an author whose book they have read. The **letter format** can also be used concerning character development. Students may write letters to a literary character, offering insight, advice, support, or criticism.

Assignments which require students to write **dialogue** offer many possibilities. For example, a teacher can invent an encounter (with some kind of tension) and ask students to write it as dialogue or a radio play. After a class has read *Lord of the Flies,* for example, you might ask students to write an additional scene in dialogue, a scene in which Ralph (or Jack) returns home and is reunited with his family.

Editorials or **news articles** about a significant event in a piece of prose offers plenty of opportunities for young writers. Such an assignment might be: "Write a news article or editorial for the *London Times* about the boys' rescue in *Lord of the Flies.* (Notice that the choice of an English newspaper will make it necessary for the writer to "sound" British . . . what other novels might a student study to learn more about English dialects?)

Student writers may be asked to write about one genre using still another. For example, ask students to write a **haiku** concerning the theme of Elie Wiesel's book *Night,* or have them write poetic epitaphs for Piggy and Simon in *Lord of the Flies* modeled after samples from *Spoon River Anthology.* Robert Frost's *"Out, Out!"* may become an obituary entry or a television news report.

WRITING ACROSS THE CURRICULUM

Teachers in all subject areas are discovering writing as a learning tool for students in their classrooms. The following describes writing assignments for a variety of subject areas, assignments which have worked successfully for teachers who believe students must write to learn.

POINT OF VIEW OR PERSONA

Specifying voice or persona is helpful in writing assignments in many academic areas. Often we ask students to write reports, and then are dismayed to discover students have copied these reports from books and encyclopedias. In a science class, for example, a report about a particular animal might be told from the animal's point of view, an assignment requiring original thought on the part of the writer. A history report about a famous person could be told from the point of view of that figure. Math students may be asked to create a conversation with a famous mathematician. By specifying point of view, you can discourage plagiarism and encourage creative, independent thinking.

EXPLANATION

Being able to explain an idea or concept requires that students get the idea clearly in mind. Writing about ideas helps students clarify their thoughts.

HISTORY—Research into the plague of the Middle Ages can be written in the form of a letter from one who is caring for the sick and dying. Copying from the encyclopedia won't work, but an understanding of the material is essential. Writing allows the student to present that understanding in a fresh, personal way.

MATH—Students write to explain a key concept or to show how two concepts are related.

SCIENCE—Students plan a lesson, a demonstration, or an experiment. The written plan becomes an explanation of a concept.

BIOLOGY—Students demonstrate their understanding of the immune system by writing letters from an antibody to an intruder, for example.

ANALYSIS

PHYSICAL EDUCATION—Students analyze in writing how a game would change if rules were altered in a specified way.

SCIENCE OR HISTORY—Reports on important people focus on *why* they were able to achieve their accomplishments.

INDUSTRIAL ARTS—Students write analyses of shop safety rules, complete with anecdotes to prove their validity.

INVENTION

MATH—Students write their own story problems, sometimes basing them on newspaper ads. Fables involving geometric principals result in fanciful mathematical tales with a point.

FOREIGN LANGUAGES—Students write cumulative stories. Each student adds a sentence or two to the story. This requires students to read and understand what they have received before they invent their addition.

SCIENCE—Students use a science fiction format to do stories on forms of energy.

INTROSPECTION

PHYSICAL EDUCATION—Students compare their fitness at the beginning and end of the program. They may have some objective data to work with, but much of the comparison may be about how they feel about themselves.

PROCESS

MATH—Students describe a mathematical process for a particular audience (fifth grade students or a parent, for example).

IMMERSION WRITING—Some teachers develop extensive units around a particular topic.

SOCIAL STUDIES—Students do considerable research on a topic and contribute to a class newspaper that includes the standard newspaper sections. The topic may be either contemporary or from an historic time period.

JOURNALS—Students track their learning experiences by noting content (who, what, where, when, and how) and ideas and their own personal response, commenting on their likes and dislikes, what they did or did not understand, and what questions they need answered.

ANY CLASS—Students keep summary journals. During the last five minutes of the class, students summarize what they have learned during that class period or write a particular number of "I Learned" statements. For makeup work, students may take turns summarizing class activities in a special class notebook. Each entry includes the date and a description of the class' activities and assignments. When absent students return, they consult the notebook. Another option is to begin each class by having the writer read his or her summary from the day before.

PHYSICAL EDUCATION, MUSIC, ART—Students write commentaries on sports events, concerts, or exhibits they have attended.

ALL CLASSES—Records of field trips, including setting goals, noting details, observing, raising questions, and evaluating learning.

FREEWRITING

ALL SUBJECTS—This writing activity functions as a preliminary activity. Students may be asked to write "all you know about _____." The writing allows you to assess the students' present knowledge at the beginning of a lesson or unit.

ALL CLASSES USING DISCUSSION—Students are asked to write freely about an idea for three to five minutes before a discussion begins. Students focus their thinking as they write and are better able to contribute to the ensuing discussion.

Teachers in all disciplines are concerned about the matter of grading. Instead of "correcting," work toward responding to ideas. Also understand that correctness is not much of an issue in some kinds of writing (journals or summaries) in contrast to others where correctness is significant (published work, letters to real people or contest entries). More and more, writing is being viewed as a legitimate learning activity and an integral part of every subject area. In classrooms across the curriculum, students are writing to learn.

APPENDIX C

WORD PROCESSING

More word processing programs are available than ever before. Tutorials abound for such projects as narrative writing, character sketches, or opinion papers. An outpouring of software intended to teach outlining, spelling, vocabulary, or editing is on the market. However, the computer and the programs alone cannot teach writing. In fact, while studies seem to suggest that young writers often produce longer documents and revise more frequently with a word processor, their revisions still tend to be superficial changes dealing only with surface errors. However, in combination with an emphasis on the writing process, the word processor has the potential to be a powerful tool and an exciting addition to the writing classroom.

When students have access to word processors in the classroom or in a writing lab, they never have to recopy an entire draft. This means that teachers can reasonably set higher final copy standards. Traditionally, teachers most often responded to errors which students could correct without recopying an entire draft and tended to ignore organizational problems which required still more drafts. In fact, requesting a second or third draft was generally found to be unproductive because students often became frustrated and made additional errors in the next draft. With the word processor, teachers may respond to the development of the student's ideas while consistently reinforcing a sense of audience. Words, sentences, or paragraphs are easily added, changed, rearranged, or deleted. Most important, the student has a record of each draft, a concrete reminder of the writing process, a process which involves temporary structures that can be changed easily.

Ideally, word processing is a tool which will help you encourage students to take greater responsibility for assessing problems in their own writing. Many teachers report that students have an improved attitude toward writing, at least partially because of the word processor. Students consider writing less frightening and punitive, and because the final draft looks more professional, many enthusiastically share it outside the classroom.

How Word Processing Can Help

The following activities are examples of how the word processor may be used to reinforce teaching of the writing process.

PREWRITING ACTIVITIES whose goals are to gather and develop ideas, organize thoughts and ideas, and generate vocabulary.

> **Word Chain:** This activity is intended to generate vocabulary and fluency and may be done on paper or with the word processor, with individual students or teams of two or three students. They begin with a four-letter word and change one letter at each step to create a new word. The individual or team with the most words wins. A sample word chain might look like this:

some	fame	lake	maps
home	lame	make	saps
hole	same	rake	taps
hale	came	rape	tars
sale	cake	nape	mars
pale	fake	tape	mark
tale	take	cape	park
tame	sake	caps	lark

An advantage of word processing is the opportunity for peer collaboration. Several parties can view the text at once and handwriting is never a problem. Collaborating is both a useful writing activity and a way to take advantage of a limited number of computers.

Chain Writing: One student begins a writing. When you indicate, another student continues. Several students may contribute to a draft. This activity focuses attention on the organization underlying a piece of writing and helps students become aware of the use of transition words, such as "first," "next," "however," and "therefore." Using this same concept, you can plan a whole class composition in which each student adds at least one sentence. Another option is to have students write a consecutive story in which the transition words are "fortunately" and "unfortunately." Still another approach is to ask each student to write about a memorable experience, but the first student stops in the middle, and a second student, who doesn't know the ending, completes the story.

Sentence Expansion: This activity is designed to focus the student's attention on descriptive language. The student first types a simple sentence. Using the word processor's ability to insert text, the student expands the sentence by adding descriptive words and phrases. The student is encouraged to fill the entire screen with a single expanded sentence. Partners may take turns adding words or phrases.

> Example: The floor creaked.
> The wooden floor creaked under my feet.
> The wooden floor, splintered and worn,
> creaked under my bare feet.

Freewriting: The word processor is an ideal tool for freewriting. One variation of freewriting possible with the word processor is "invisible writing." The monitor is turned off or the brightness is turned down so no characters appear on the screen during the typing. This frees the writer to focus on ideas without concentrating on text errors.

DRAFTING ACTIVITIES whose goal is to record a complete, unedited version of a writing.

Freewriting: Freewriting may become a first draft. Changes for second and third drafts easily follow, and the changes may be complex, involving moving or deleting entire paragraphs.

Screenstory: The teacher provides a first and last sentence such as "Her alarm clock rang" and "She got out of bed." The first and last lines are placed at the top of the monitor. The student begins by placing the cursor between the two sentences and the story is expanded to fill up the screen of the monitor but can be no longer than that.

News Story: In this activity, a student assumes the role of newspaper reporter. The editor wants a copy of the first draft in ten minutes. Using a "fact card" with the basic information for the story supplied by the teacher and a knowledge of news writing, the student produces a first draft. As editor, the teacher may later supply additional information as the news "breaks" or call for "rewrites."

EDITING ACTIVITIES whose goals are to improve the first drafts and produce a final polished version of the writing.

> Word processors allow a writer to play with lines,
> insert, delete, and move long passages. It isn't
> possible to count revisions, because they take
> place simultaneously with the generation of text.

Peer evaluation: Student writers frequently work in pairs. With peer evaluation, the writing receives more immediate, concentrated, and energetic feedback than an individual teacher could possibly give. Students can swap disks and comment right on other student's disks, using caps, boldface, or brackets to show the changed text.

PUBLISHING ACTIVITIES whose goal is to produce writing which looks professional and which can be shared outside the classroom.

> Students may produce class booklets, personal
> booklets, anthologies of short stories or poems,
> or class newspapers or magazines. Like profes-
> sional writers, students feel pride in authorship.
> Aware of an audience, they revise more will-
> ingly and look forward to writing again.

The computer as a writing tool offers exciting possibilities for teachers because it encourages play and experimentation. It makes rewriting easier and forgives mistakes. Most important, it thoroughly supports the teaching of writing as a process.

Bibliography

Applebee, Arthur N. "Looking at Writing," *Educational Leadership* (March 1981), p. 458.

Atwell, Nancy. *In the Middle: Writing, Reading, and Learning with Adolescents.* Montclair, NJ: Boynton/Cook, 1987.

Calkins, Lucy McCormick. *The Art of Teaching Writing.* Portsmouth, NH: Heinemann, 1986.

Campbell, David. *Take the Road to Creativity. . . .* Niles, IL: Argus Communications, 1977.

Canfield, Jack and Well, Harold C. *100 Ways to Enhance Self-Concept in the Classroom.* Englewood Cliffs, NJ: Prentice Hall, 1976.

Caplan, Rebekah. *Writers in Training.* Palo Alto, CA: Dale Seymour Publications, 1984.

Diederich, Paul. *Measuring Growth in Writing.* Urbana, IL: NCTE, 1974.

Elbow, Peter. *Writing with Power.* New York: Oxford University Press, 1981.

Emig, Janet. *The Web of Meaning.* Montclair, NJ: Boynton/Cook, 1983.

Fisher, B. Aubrey. *Small Group Decision Making: Communication and the Group Process.* New York: McGraw-Hill, 1974.

Geuder, Patricia; Harvey, Linda; Denis, Lloyd L.; and Wages, Jack, eds. *They Really Taught Us How to Write.* Urbana, IL: NCTE, 1974.

Graves, Donald. *Teachers and Children at Work.* Portsmouth, NH: Heinemann, 1984.

Henderson, Kathy. *Market Guide for Young Writers.* Belvidere, NJ: Shoe Tree Press, 1988.

Murray, Donald M. *A Writer Teaches Writing: A Practical Method of Teaching Composition.* Boston: Houghton Mifflin, 1968.

NCTE Commission on Composition. "Teaching Composition: A Position Statement," *College English* (October 1974), pp. 210–220.

Rico, Gabriele. *Writing the Natural Way.* Los Angeles: J. P. Tarcher, Inc., 1983.

Romano, Tom. *Clearing the Way: Working with Teenage Writers.* Portsmouth, NH: Heinemann, 1987.

Rosenshine, Barak and Furst, Norma. "Research on Teacher Performance Criteria," *Research in Teacher Education.* Englewood Cliffs, NJ: Prentice Hall, 1971.

Sherwin, J. Stephen. *Four Problems in Teaching English: A Critique of Research.* Urbana, IL: NCTE, 1969.

"Standards for Basic Skills Writing Programs," *Slate Newsletter,* I (April 1979), p. 1.

Walshe, R. D. "What's Basic to Teaching Writing?" *English Journal* (December 1979), pp. 51–56.

Whitehead, Frank. *Creative Experiment*. London: Chatto and Windus, 1970.

Wisconsin Writing Project. *A Guide to Evaluating Student Writing*. Madison: University of Wisconsin Press, 1978.

Wisconsin Writing Project. *A Guide to Using the Journal*. Madison: University of Wisconsin Press, 1983.